T0149186

INTO HELL

INTO HELL

★ ★ ★

Hugo Sims' Story of Normandy,
Holland & Bastogne

By
Herb Moore

authorHOUSE®

AuthorHouse™
1663 Liberty Drive
Bloomington, IN 47403
www.authorhouse.com
Phone: 1 (800) 839-8640

© 2015 Herb Moore. All rights reserved.

No part of this book may be reproduced, stored in a retrieval system, or transmitted by any means without the written permission of the author.

Published by AuthorHouse 10/23/2015

ISBN: 978-1-5049-5427-3 (sc)
ISBN: 978-1-5049-5426-6 (e)

Library of Congress Control Number: 2015916361

Print information available on the last page.

Any people depicted in stock imagery provided by Thinkstock are models, and such images are being used for illustrative purposes only. Certain stock imagery © Thinkstock.

This book is printed on acid-free paper.

Because of the dynamic nature of the Internet, any web addresses or links contained in this book may have changed since publication and may no longer be valid. The views expressed in this work are solely those of the author and do not necessarily reflect the views of the publisher, and the publisher hereby disclaims any responsibility for them.

Contents

FOREWORD

I first met Hugo Sims when he arrived at Camp Toccoa to train as a paratrooper in March of 1943. He was assigned to my unit for training in the 101st Airborne Division, the 501st PIR. I was skeptical at first, due to the fact that he was very short and extremely undersized for the paratrooper duties I knew he would face. I had my Lt. Rice take Hugo and about twenty other candidates out for an extended run to test their endurance and ability to continue. I told Lt. Rice to run until the men dropped out. I don't remember how far they ran, but at the conclusion, the only two remaining were Lt. Rice and Hugo Sims. I knew right then Hugo had what it took to excel.

Hugo Sims and I went through World War II together, from Normandy to Operation Market Garden in Holland, and then through the Battle of the Bulge in Bastogne. Hugo demonstrated every characteristic of a strong leader. He showed that in each battle we fought. His true leadership was exposed to the world when he led a patrol deep behind German lines to capture a prisoner when our forces had little information about the German forces we faced. That patrol was written up in *Life Magazine* as the Incredible Patrol and put the 101st

Airborne on the map. It also won him the Distinguished Service Cross, the second highest medal our country can award. At Bastogne, he exposed himself to German fire time and time again, running from headquarters to the front lines and back, in order to gather information, which ultimately led to his promotion to Company Commander. Later in France he won the Silver Star for leading his company against a German unit over twice the size of his company in a night assault.

I have commanded thousands of military men in many battles during my career through three wars. If I were faced with deciding on one man I would want to be by my side in combat, that man would be Hugo Sims.

Brigadier General Richard J. Allen, Sr.,
U.S. Army (Retired)

INTRODUCTION

This is the story of Hugo S. Sims and his experiences during World War II. As a 20-year-old senior track team star at Wofford College in Spartanburg, SC, Sims volunteered to join the Army. His application for Officer Candidate School was rejected and after graduation he began training as a Private at Camp Wheeler, Georgia. Upon learning that Sims had been turned down on his attempt to attend Officer Candidate School on his first application, his superior officer in basic training obtained an additional review. Sims passed this review and was commissioned a Second Lieutenant in the Army. He applied for and was accepted into the paratroopers and was sent to Toccoa, Georgia, for training.

His story discloses that Hugo Sims was not just another paratrooper passing through the military. Each encounter with obstacles and difficult assignments demonstrated his leadership and bravery. Sims was not flamboyant and flashy. His low-key demeanor could easily have been misinterpreted. He was never indecisive when the battles began.

I spent three years interviewing Hugo one-on-one. Slowly, but definitively the true warrior surfaced. He was reluctant to tell his part in any action at first. I shifted tactics and interviewed others who were there with Hugo, such as Brigadier General Richard Allen, in order to delve deeper into my Hugo research. Upon the continuation of my sessions with Hugo, he loosened up and started to give more information in answering questions.

My conversations with Hugo over those three years evolved into a lifelong friendship with him. I was honored to call him a friend and awed by his service as a member of the 101st Airborne Division. You may see some deviations from strict literary form in this narrative. I quoted what Hugo told me, and then switched to past tense in order to tell the story to the reader. I hope the reader will excuse my literary indulgences.

There were others who had a part in the telling of Hugo's story. My wife, Kathy, corrected my manuscript multiple times to fix everything from content to misplaced punctuation marks, then advised me what to rewrite or fix. She deserves any and all credit for the readability I missed. No professional editor could do a better job. My thanks will never be enough for her work.

Hugo's family played a vital role. His wife, Virginia, supported the entire project and process. She put up with our conferences and meetings for years. His children, Hugo III, Cal, and Ginger were also constantly positive and offered that same level of support. Of course, they already knew the Hugo I would come to understand and have the benefit of getting to know.

Brig. General Richard Allen was a vital link to Hugo Sims' wartime service. I was fortunate to have him consent to probing questions regarding Hugo and their years of service together. General Allen gave me several pictures dating back to the 501ˢᵗ training days I had never seen. As he and I talked about those WWII days, I more clearly understood what went into the making of a paratrooper and how that training produced results from Normandy all the way through Bastogne. We talked as we sat in his office in Atlanta, surrounded by memorabilia from his years of military service, including the cricket he carried as he jumped into Normandy. His respect for Hugo Sims was evident as we talked.

Mark Bando, author of many books and publications, is also the historian of the 101ˢᵗ Airborne Division. Included in this book are pictures and other items he graciously provided to me during the telling of Hugo's story. He redirected my research many times in an effort to make certain that I had access to and included the most credible information. Thanks, Mark.

The Dwight D. Eisenhower website provided facts, as well as battle maps as did the www.101airborneww2.com website. The www.army.mil/cmh website was not only an interesting read, but a constant source of reference material through the entire writing of Hugo's story. The January 15, 1945 issue of *Life Magazine* in which Hugo's Incredible Patrol was featured provided additional information.

I took a research trip to France so I could see and touch the places Hugo passed through. I stood at Hell's Corner and immediately understood the fear of an ambush by an enemy. There is no place to hide for cover and/or concealment there. I walked across the LaBarquette Lock and saw how vital that spot was to the flooding of the areas behind Utah Beach. I met the family now living in the lockkeeper's house and walked down to the barn. It was all much the same as it was in 1944. The flat land surrounding the lock was just as Hugo described it; easy to defend if one occupied it and difficult to take if one was to capture the lock. I walked over to the approximate point where Hugo landed in the water that night of invasion. In daylight it looked calm and sedate. At night with German machine guns firing away and not knowing where the enemy was, it had to be horrible. That trip opened my eyes to many things the Allies faced; the N-13 Highway so exposed where Allies had to cross open space in the advance to Carentan, the rising terrain towards Addeville and St. Come-Du-Mont, the railroad bridges that had to be captured beside the N-13, the Douvre River bridges over open marshland and low delta land that impeded attackers. All the features, plus a visit to the cemetery at Normandy where all those crosses so perfectly lined up in formation brought home the knowledge that those of us who were not there will never, never really know what our servicemen faced and conquered on June 6, 1944.

Throughout the entire process a common thread kept surfacing; Hugo Sims was much more than the ordinary man casual acquaintances thought they knew. He was a man of purpose, a man with moral and steadfast faith and courage. He showed those characteristics throughout his entire life. We could all take lessons from that life.

D-DAY

NORMANDY

THAT FIRST JUNE NIGHT

"To know how to wait is the great secret of success"
- Xavier de Maistre

The C-47's flew southwest toward their marker boat stationed off the northwest tip of the Cotentin Peninsula of France. The planes had lifted off English soil at 2221 hours, 10:21 pm, and climbed to 2000 feet. Approaching the English Channel, the aircraft dipped to flying altitude for the trip over the water. This altitude of five hundred feet placed them below the probing eyes of German radar. The moon was nearly full, casting a deep purple-blue-black tint to the channel below and punctuating frothy whitecaps in the water. Winds were brisk, out of the west at 35 mph.

The flight plan was to swing southeast at the marker boat, then dash east into French airspace after passing the small islands of Guernsey and Jersey. This path would take the planes into drop zones from west to east, arriving behind German lines and fortifications on the beaches of Normandy. The Allied Command had code named Utah, Omaha, Juno, Sword and Gold Beaches on the coast and identified them as assault targets. Their specific Drop

Zone (DZ) was behind Utah Beach, where the Army's 4th Infantry Division was to storm ashore at daybreak. The prearranged flight path placed the aircraft over the drop zones for less than ten minutes, plenty of time to complete their part in the overall plan.

Twin 1,200 horsepower Pratt & Whitney R-1830-S1C3G Twin Wasp radial piston engines droned in the night, powering each aircraft at the normal cruising speed of just under two hundred miles an hour. For paratroop operations, the C-47 interior was fitted with 28 fold-down bucket seats hinged to the walls. Six parachute containers filled with explosives and equipment for use on the ground were on some planes, attached to racks under the fuselage and ready for release by the pilots once over the proper drop zones. Painted olive drab for the military, the 1,000 transports were marked with three white and two black bands around the fuselage and each wing for easy recognition and identification in flight.

Wind buffeted the C-47's with sufficient velocity to cause sudden lurches up and down, as well as side-to-side. Paratroopers of the 501st Parachute Infantry Regiment (PIR) sat in the darkness, helmet-clad heads bobbing in unison with the motion of the bumps of the invisible air currents outside. Darkness enveloped the interior of the transport, except for the small pale blue light in the tiny passageway to the pilot's compartment. This faint glow afforded modest details of faces sitting in the semi-darkness, but there was an element of apprehension in all the men. They tried, as do all men heading towards danger, to show a game face. Some sat with helmet-clad heads resting against the bulkhead of the plane, eyes closed. Others sat staring at nothing; eyes open but unseen by others in the dark shadows, thinking about the operation, or home, or whether or not they would survive until daylight. With the aircraft bouncing and swaying as it was, some even wondered to themselves if the plane would hold together long enough to get them to the drop zone.

The jumpmaster stood near the open door with a major and one young lieutenant; all three staring down at the black water below. Other C-47's, over a thousand of them, full of more paratroopers from the 101st, 82nd Airborne, and the British 6th Airborne were flying in multiple V formations in the dark sky, like so many geese heading south in October. Over 17,000 paratroopers were staged for the night jump. As the planes passed midpoint of the English channel, the jumpmaster and two officers saw thousands of ships on the water, all heading southward toward the largest beach assault invasion ever attempted in history: D-Day, Operation Overlord, the day the Allies invaded France at the previously unheralded Normandy beaches.

Inside those outwardly tranquil ships floating below on the water were hundreds of thousands of men armed with the most modern weapons of destruction: bazookas, Bangelor torpedoes, flame throwers, hand grenades, rifle grenades, 30 and 50 caliber machine guns, tanks, wheel mounted artillery and tons upon tons of ammo and explosive charges. Men inside those ships were charged with the task of winning the beaches first, and then plunging headlong toward the heart of the German held territories in France, Holland, and Belgium. The plan called for them to destroy Hitler's army and liberate those countries viciously invaded under Hitler's orders. History was to be written in the coming weeks, a history to change the world. The veteran sergeant and two officers watched the ships for a few minutes, and then peered back into the solemn and dark confines of the plane.

The 501st PIR was part of the 101st Airborne Division. Colonel Howard F. "Skeet" Johnson, a demanding and hardened veteran who trained his men to excel at physical conditioning and the determination to succeed in combat, led the 501st. An Annapolis graduate from Washington, DC, he had trained alongside his troops, often making three or four jumps to each one made by his men. Paratroopers of the 501st affectionately switched his nickname to "Jumpy" instead of "Skeet" as a result of his love to parachute with the Airborne. He had been a young lieutenant colonel when he enrolled in the parachute school located at Fort Benning, Georgia and earned the coveted wings of a paratrooper.

Colonel Jumpy Johnson was an angular man, thin and sinewy, with blonde hair and clear eyes, filled with a passion to excel. Men shuddered under his demands when his anger exploded and his fiery eyes gleamed intensely. Demanding and precise, Colonel Johnson was charged with molding the raw recruits, which he handpicked, into a force to be reckoned with in any situation. He was not interested in average. His men had to be much more than that. He would personally see to it himself. Johnson knew that men had to be filled with total commitment if they were to be the best. Total commitment meant they had to obey orders instantly, without hesitation and with complete trust in their leaders. Each individual would be tested to ensure he had that extra drive to be one of Johnson's men.

One factor high on Johnson's list was the attitude of each man under his command. He had to know they would do whatever was necessary in any situation. He had to be completely satisfied that the men would do the impossible. Could they go without rest? Did they have the guts? Did they have the desire? Could they exist on almost nothing and still succeed? Above all, could they actually kill? It was one thing to sit on a ship far out at sea and send huge artillery rounds into an unseen enemy, killing at random, or drop bombs from high altitudes and return to a warm bed at night, knowing that you had just killed someone. But it was another thing altogether to look a man in the eye and deliberately put a bullet in his face, or, in the absence of a firearm, to grasp a man with bare hands, pull out a knife and slit his throat, then watch the life ooze from him, feeling his warm blood drip down your arms and hands in the process. Unacceptable in civilian life, that very trait could mean the difference between being a survivor or a dead body. Dead bodies won no battles. Johnson did not want to risk that possibility.

Jumpy Johnson led the men on conditioning runs, pushing and cajoling them to run faster and farther than on the previous run, then do it in less time. He led them in calisthenics, again pushing them to extremes and teaching them how to do more with less. His training camp was the outdoors, knowing that the outdoors would be their home in combat. No frills and no nonsense. Bare bones comforts and rigid training were the order of the day for anyone who wanted to become a paratrooper with Johnson. Everywhere they went, they ran. Johnson weeded out those who couldn't keep up with the tough schedule. If they couldn't keep up in training, they would fail in combat. Johnson knew that. He wasn't willing to be surrounded by anyone who would give up.

Camp Toccoa became the dusty, dirty home to those who trained for the 501st. Scratched out of red Georgia clay, Toccoa was not much more than wooden shacks with tarpaper roofs. When it rained, the Georgia clay turned into a quagmire of slippery gummy mud that stuck to boots and clothes with a stubborn determination to make training even more miserable. The recruits ran up and down a famous nearby hill called Currahee so much that the very mention of that name conjured up memories of desperation and exhaustion. They ran in the cold, ran in the rain and mud, ran in lightweight running clothes, and ran in full combat gear. They carried their weapons, carried additional weight to simulate extra ammo that would be carried in combat, and they carried each other on obstacle courses. Leg muscles ached every night. There was no end to the conditioning in those winter and spring months at Toccoa. Slowly, sometimes in agony, they whipped themselves into shape. By the time Toccoa was behind them, they were a reflection of their leader, lean and fit, ready and prepared to meet the next challenge. Many did not survive the weeding out process. As few as thirty men out of every hundred remained when the training at Toccoa was completed.

The early months of 1943 molded the 501st into a fighting unit under the stern eyes of a commander they would all grow to love and respect. Moving first to Fort Benning for four weeks of parachute school, then to North Carolina, and on to Tennessee, the 501st completed training and was declared ready to join the fighting overseas. Colonel Johnson was eager to get going. Training was over. Time to go to work.

Someone near the front of one C-47 got airsick, throwing up in a small bucket passed around for that purpose. The small pink pills for airsickness didn't always work, especially in a plane bouncing around in the clutches of high winds. Many had taken several doses of the pills. The trip was to take two hours. Some thought the pills would help them catch a few winks of sleep during the flight. Didn't work. Stomachs churned, if not from airsickness, from nerves. If the airsickness and nerves weren't the cause, it was apprehension, or fear or anticipation. After all, they were headed into the unknown. This was the first combat for the 501st. No matter the training, no matter the preparation and classes, for the most part, none knew what was ahead. The odor of vomit drifted in the air, mixed with a hint of exhaust fumes from the propellers churning away outside. The noise of the motors rose and fell as pilots attempted to keep a tight formation, urging the aircraft up or down, sometimes left or right, adding to the discomfort of the paratroopers.

Inside one C-47 was a young lieutenant of the 501st, bouncing around like those sitting on each side of the transport plane. He stood with Major Richard Allen, his CO, at the open door of the aircraft, alongside the veteran jumpmaster sergeant. As the Assistant G-3 of his regiment, First Lieutenant Hugo Sims would be the last out the door over the DZ. His parachute harness and his gear were securely strapped in place and his mussette bag packed with spare clothes, hand grenades, hand shovel, mess kit, rifle cleaning kit, compass, maps, toiletries, two extra pairs of socks, a picture of his wife, French money, and first aid gear.

Hugo Sims recalled, "I didn't want to carry the extra weight so I shoved some chocolate bars into my pockets for food and tossed the balance of the K-rations before we took-off." He wasn't going to starve without the K-rations; " I just figured the chocolate would be enough. I carried a carbine in a canvas bag strapped across my chest and two .45 pistols on a cartridge belt."

Sims had more gear, including his gas mask, attached to other pieces of equipment,. Jump gloves fit snugly and his knife was holstered in the sheath of his combat boots. The Mae West life preserver was strapped tightly to his upper torso. His body weight was less than a hundred thirty pounds. His gear weighed as much as he did. He had packed his chute like the other paratroopers. Face darkened by charcoal, he was as prepared as he could be for whatever followed. Impatient to get on the ground and start on his assigned target, he could only sit and wait. All in due time, Hugo Sims was to become a combat veteran.

The young lieutenant was a graduate of Wofford College in South Carolina. Sims was born, raised, and educated in Orangeburg, South Carolina, a small town midway between the capital city of Columbia and the coastal town of Charleston. Just like most of the South, Orangeburg sweltered in the summer. Most locals found little to smile about during those days following the Depression years. A rural, farming community inhabited by hard working modest people, Orangeburg was sending her young soldiers off to war. It wasn't easy to watch them board buses and trains, not knowing if, or when, they would return. However, Orangeburg wasn't the type of community to question Washington's decisions. Patriotic loyalty and commitment were well known characteristics of the citizens. It was a time of concern and prayer for those young men sent into the wrath of war.

Sims's lean figure and quiet manner hid a fierce competitor. His physical stamina had earned him a spot on the Wofford track team, and he could run for hours on end. Sims refused to quit any race, winning more than his fair share in competition on sheer determination. He recalled, "I worked hard to stayed in good physical condition. I ran ten miles every day during the summer before going to college. I maintained a steady training schedule of running from that point on."

After graduating from college, Sims married his high school sweetheart, Virginia; he called her "Gin." Still does. Sims recalled, "I wrote columns for my father's news syndicate and I continued to do that until I graduated." Sims became quite the accomplished wordsmith while still a student. "The syndicate was growing and I believed I would continue in my father's footsteps to grow and expand the business."

"Then," Sims spoke in a lower tone, " Japan attacked Pearl Harbor in 1941." Sims knew his fate; he would join the fighting forces and prepare for war. He volunteered, not knowing what was in his future, but confident of his ability to face whatever came his way. "I signed up for the US Army and was sent to Camp Wheeler, where I sought a commission as an officer." Turned down as an Officer Candidate School applicant by the review committee, Sims was puzzled as to why he was not accepted. "They only told me I had not passed the board evaluation." It only deepened his resolve to prove they were wrong. He had few options. "I could stay in the army as a private, or enter another branch of service. I chose to remain and completed basic training."

Three months later, Sims's commanding officer thought the review committee had made a mistake with Sims. He arranged for Sims to get another meeting with the review board under new officers. This time Sims passed without question. They offered the opinion that Sims would make an excellent officer. Sims left for OCS at Fort Benning, Georgia.

Sims remembered, "Halfway through OCS training, it was announced that two candidates, out my class of two hundred, would be selected to become paratroopers. When I heard about the paratroopers, I knew where I wanted to go." Thirty men applied. Two were selected. Sims was one.

"Captain Richard Allen, of Atlanta, Georgia, was my Company Commander," Sims smiled. Allen had no idea that this soft-spoken, slightly built, southern gentleman could run right alongside his trusted and hardened Lt.

Rice, step for step. Allen planned a grueling run to weed out the new lieutenant who he thought was too small to pass all the rigors to come. He ordered Rice to run as many miles as it took for Sims to quit.

Sims remembered that test well, "We started out with the platoon of about thirty-five men. At the conclusion of the run, the only ones left were Lt. Rice and me." Sims was promoted to First Lieutenant and became a leader in the company, later being promoted to a staff position under Major Allen.

Sims was Assistant G-3 of the 501st PIR. He studied the plan for his part in the invasion. His unit was to take and hold La Barquette lock on the Douve River, south of the small village of Vierville, and to destroy both highway bridges crossing the Douve. Overall plans developed by the high command looked good on paper. It was a well-designed plan that could produce the desired end result if all went well. Lieutenant Sims went over his assignment in his mind as the flight continued in the rough air over the Channel. His stomach tightened like the others. The unknown always harbored apprehension, and each man was touched by unspoken and sometimes unthinkable fears of what may await him in the dark night in France.

"The flight over was bumpy," Sims remembered. "It was real quiet in our plane. Nobody talked much and most everyone just sat and thought. Richard Allen and I talked a little but we couldn't hear much over the noise of the plane."

The C-47 tilted left in a sweeping turn heading southeast. They had reached the marker boat. Only a few minutes more and they would pass by the tiny islands off the western coast of France. Then the planes would proceed inland, passing over the coast. Each man knew the procedure. The red light by the exit door of the plane would come on. That was the signal for the jumpmaster to shout the order, "STAND UP AND HOOK UP." A cable strung down the center of the cargo bay was used to attach the metal snap of the static line. This fifteen-foot static line was a strap attached to the flap on the parachute pack strapped on each back. A reserve chute was in a separate harness strapped across each paratrooper's chest. When a paratrooper jumped from the plane, the static line tightened and jerked open the flap on the parachute pack. If, for any reason, the main parachute failed to deploy, the paratrooper could yank a ripcord and deploy the reserve chute.

Once standing, each man checked the harness and gear of the man in front of him. Upon command, each man, starting with the man closest to the pilot, would shout out "NUMBER 17, OK." The next man in the single file line would shout "NUMBER 16, OK," the next would shout "NUMBER 15, OK," and on down the line until the man nearest the door was checked out. The jumpmaster would give the command, "STAND IN THE DOOR," and the men would snug up to each other behind the man nearest the door, ready to jump. Over the proper DZ, when the green light came on, the jumpmaster would shove out the equipment packs on the plane floor that would support the troops on the ground, then shout, "GO!" as jumpers plunged out the door into the darkness one at a time behind the lead jumper.

Sims silently reviewed the procedure for jumping. "Hold your head down." "Arms tight across the reserve chute on the chest." "Feet 8 inches apart." "Check the canopy." "Get the wind at your back." "Pull the risers to maneuver." "Don't lock your knees." "Dropping too fast, pull the reserve." Silently repeating the procedure added a measure of confidence in the darkness. They had done it many times. Repetition had made the procedure almost automatic. Still, it didn't hurt to go over it in your mind again. The DZ was drawing nearer.

Each C-47 carried a full contingent of paratroopers, called a "stick." Sims recalled the facts, "No matter the number of troopers in any one aircraft, the paratroopers as a whole were called a stick. Some sticks had twenty men. Sometimes, a stick consisted of only twelve or fourteen men. The number varied. Some sticks were full squads, while others could be made up of a combination of men with different jobs. Sometimes a company or battalion staff officer loaded in with a particular squad to fill out a stick." While there may be twenty-eight seats, rarely could twenty-eight fully equipped paratroopers fit on those small seats. Some troopers were so bulkily loaded down they sat or kneeled on the floor of the aircraft and rested their parachute and pack on the seats. Some found it easier to stand, holding on to the static-line cable or the steel members of the plane's superstructure.

The pitch sound of the engines increased. The nose of the aircraft lifted perceptibly up at an angle, indicating an increase in altitude as they approached the coastline. Mouths dried like cotton. Hands became clammy, even inside jump gloves. Faces felt suddenly warm. Pilots watched their formation closely. For the most part they were rookies on their first combat drop too.

To avoid small arms fire, the C-47's would climb to 1500 feet as they passed over the French coast. Once they cleared the coast, the plan called for them to drop back down to 700 feet and reduce the airspeed from 180 to 100 mph for the drop. They would look for the proper indicator ground markings to identify the correct drop zones and flash on the green light for the jump. Equipment packs would go out first, then the men.

Other paratroopers, the pathfinders, had jumped an hour earlier. They parachuted with equipment lights and a new radar system to mark the different drop zones so the pilots could see when to switch on the green jump light. Some drop zones would be marked with white lights, some with blue, some with timed flashing white lights, like two short flashes. Some would be marked with the new radar sets. In reality, they were much like a modern day garage door opener. The unit on the ground was a static unit, doing nothing until the pilot pressed a button in the plane. At that point, the ground unit sent out an answering signal that could be read and followed to the proper drop zone. The plan was well conceived and there was no indication the pathfinders had not completed their task. All looked OK as the planes gained altitude.

Lead pilots saw the coastline below and turned on the red light. "STAND UP AND HOOK UP," came the jumpmaster's loud command. It was time. They were ready to bail out into the unknown. Following the order, paratroopers started the final preparations they had practiced so often. They went through the equipment checks, sounded off the readiness of each man, and then crowded towards the open door, ready to jump. Just as the pilots felt a glow of confidence, things began to unravel. And it got worse by the minute.

The first indication of danger appeared. Along the French coast flight path, clouds, or a very high and dense fog enveloped the planes. Pilots could not see the aircraft next to them in the formation. As taught in flight school, the pilots turned and shifted their plane's position to get extra space between the aircraft, thereby avoiding a potential midair collision. Mistake number one.

Next came distant "thump" and "whomp" sounds of muffled explosions. Flak. It arrived first in muted seemingly distant flashes. Then as it grew closer, the sounds grew from the muffled sound of a bad exhaust system backfire on a car to ear-splitting red, white, and yellow explosions, spewing shrapnel into the air and onto the planes, shaking and rocking the aircraft. The sky filled with more explosions and rookie pilots took evasive actions, tilting and turning their aircraft, dispersing the formations further. Mistake number two.

Machine gun fire arrived with tracer rounds zipping up in curved arcs, searching for random hits on the noisy planes flying through the clearing sky. Those tracer rounds represented every fifth bullet coming from the machine guns, which meant there were four more unseen bullets tearing through the night sky that were invisible. Red, blue, yellow and green tracers zinged and zipped past the planes, along with the "plinking" sound of shrapnel hitting the outside layer of thin metal on the aircraft. Machine gun rounds hit some aircraft, shearing through the thin sheet steel like it was paper, shattering into the bay where the paratroopers stood nervously.

Shrapnel hit some men. Machine gun fire wounded some. A few were killed before parachuting that night. The sky looked like a gigantic New Year's fireworks display outside. The sound of rounds piercing the air, and the sight of those deadly curving arcs of tracers coming up from the ground were terrifying. Those who could see through the door or windows saw strobe-like flashes of planes and black puffs of flak that disappeared as the light from the explosions blinked out. There was no escape for the paratroopers. Just get to the DZ. Hearts pulsed. Eyes bulged. Jaws tightened. Their war had arrived. D-Day was here.

Sims thought back, "Some pilots attempted more evasive moves in an attempt to avoid being hit by enemy fire." Most pilots, swerving and gaining altitude, increased their airspeed to 180 mph to make adjustments. In all the mayhem, pilots lost perspective of their designated flight plans and orders. The rookie pilots were under the influence of near panic, some frantically attempting to climb further into the night sky. Unaware, the pilots were now flying too fast and their formation had become too fragmented to recover before they reached their proper drop zones. Mistake number three.

The C-47's reduced airspeed and dropped lower. The clouds, or fog, cleared away, but the damage was done. The faster airspeed had taken them further inland than planned. To add to the confusion, the pathfinders who parachuted earlier had not achieved all their objectives. Some drop zones were not marked. Some drop zone lights had been discovered by the Germans who shot out the lights as quickly as the lights switched on. Planes were heading towards incorrect drop zones at the wrong altitude and flying excessively fast. Pilots hastily guessed at their locations, and then switched on the green jump light when they estimated they were over the correct drop zone.

During all the evasive actions of the pilots, men and equipment were tossed around in some planes like laundry tumbling wildly in a clothes dryer gone amuck. More paratroopers threw up, adding the odor of vomit to the newer smell of exploded, burnt cordite. Some equipment bags on the floor became wedged in the doorway. They had to be dislodged and shoved out the door before the men could jump. Jumpmasters struggled to get the doorway cleared; all the while the plane was flying past the drop zone. Things got worse.

Pilots decreased airspeed for the drop, but some in all the chaos were still flying too fast. Paratroopers jumped into the black night with whistling arcs of machine gun fire nipping nearby. They normally jumped at 100 mph. They found out very violently what it was like to jump at speeds near 150 mph. Instead of the hard yank of the parachute tugging open, it literally wrenched them to a dead stop in less than two seconds. It was like jumping out of a car driving 35 miles an hour and grabbing a fire hydrant. Men were knocked unconscious. Some broke arms and collarbones from the violent shock. Drop bags, bags with extra gear suspended on a line from the paratrooper's leg, were ripped off in the process, never to be recovered. Some rifles were ripped away from paratroopers, who ended up on the ground with no weapon for the fight.

Aside from the shock of the high-speed drop, another obstacle surfaced. Some planes had dropped well below the normal altitude for jumps. In the mayhem, altitudes had shifted so much that there were planes everywhere, at numerous altitudes. Men who expected to be suspended in the air for thirty or forty seconds under their chutes, from the usual altitude of 700 feet, found themselves slamming to earth almost as soon as their parachutes opened. They tore into trees, fences, ditches, canals, open fields, and buildings without time to adjust for the landing. This resulted in more broken bones and injuries in the dark. Some paratroopers died upon impact in the darkness.

Because of the higher airspeed and equipment bags lodged in the exit doorways of the planes, some paratroopers landed well past drop zones and were spread out, as one man put it, "all over Hell and half of Georgia." At those high airspeeds, each extra second of time that passed to exit the aircraft put a paratrooper another quarter mile further away from his designated drop zone. Paratroopers were spread out over an area of 300 square miles instead of the tight drop zone patterns of the plan. One unit missed their drop zone by 30 miles. Equipment packs containing food supplies, radios, extra batteries, and ammo were lost, some never recovered. Those paratroopers with radios had them secured in leg pockets or in their mussette bags. The heavier and bulkier radios were broken down into two parts, carried by two men, to be reassembled on the ground when the stick assembled. Because the drops were so spread out, many of those two-man teams never got together on the ground to reassemble the radios.

The combination of mistakes added to the confusion. The well-organized plan, along with the command structure, appeared to dissolve by the minute. All the practice, the repetition, all the effort appeared for naught. Paratroopers were spread over a corridor twenty miles long and fifteen miles wide, with little or no contact between units. They would fight in small units, sometimes with as little as one or two men. Leadership under fire would have to come from individuals, not the listed, structured officer corps in the normal military chain of command. They were spread out over too large an area. Darkness made the situation worse.

Planes were shot down, exploding in midair or twisting and spiraling in flaming turns, bursting upon ground contact. Wings separated from some, sheared off by exploding flak or multiple hits by the relentless machine guns blasting away into the night air, causing the plane to loop out of control to the ground, paratroopers and crew still onboard. The result was more horrible than most dared imagine. Death arrived before dawn and it continued. Stiff and bitter fighting would follow, some in hand-to-hand fights with knives and bare hands. The nightmare had begun.

Lt. Hugo Sims was the last man out of his plane. He flung himself into the darkness, as in those many practice jumps. At the stiff jolt of his parachute opening, Sims recalled, "I looked up to check the canopy. It was OK. C-47's filled the sky." Parachutes tossed and swung in the twilight of bursting flak and exploding aircraft.

"Some paratroopers were shot as they floated down." The wounded yelled out in pain, while the dead hung limp in their harness as they plopped to the ground in a heap. Searchlights probed the air with bright streams of white light. Tracers arched up from below, searching out individual parachutists in the firefight-light in the sky.

Once outside the planes, the sound of the machine guns grew loud and menacing. Bullets zipped by so close Sims remembered, "I tucked my legs up to avoid them." For Sims, the ground couldn't arrive soon enough, "I pulled the risers to get my back with the wind. But when I looked down, my heart skipped a beat." He saw what every paratrooper dreaded: water.

THE FIRST OBJECTIVES

"The young do not know enough to be prudent,
and therefore they attempt the impossible--and
achieve it, generation after generation."
-Pearl S. Buck

Allied Command selected the LaBarquette lock as a critical objective. The muddy Douve River passed through the lock in route to the ocean. Not more than eight feet high, the concrete rock and steel structure controlled the flow of water into the lowlands between Utah Beach and the town of Carentan, some fifteen miles inland. Left under German control, the lock could be closed to allow incoming tide river water to back up into the lowlands. If that happened, no vehicular traffic could pass beyond the limited high ground on the raised dike-like roadbeds. If that flooding took place, the 4th Infantry Division, if successful in taking Utah Beach, would be halted just beyond the sand dunes, and there would be no ready access for the Allies to attack from multiple directions. The lock at LaBarquette held the key. Whoever controlled those locks controlled the entire valley floor between Utah Beach and Carentan.

A quick capture of the La Barquette lock was essential. If the Germans counterattacked the beach assault, knowing the layout of the land and the strategic importance of the lock, they could reinforce their beach defenses and do vast damage to the assault plans of the Allies. Johnson was determined to take the lock swiftly before daylight, and had assigned the job to the First Battalion. Their DZ would place them less than two miles away from the lock. A quick strike in the darkness before sunrise would surprise any German guards at the lock. With a little luck and stealth, the Germans wouldn't even know the Americans were near before the attack.

The LaBarquette Lock sat squarely in the center of the flat lowland valley. Gentle hills gave way to the flatland below St. Come du Mont, just north of highway N-13, the main Cherbourg to Carentan route. Standing on the lock, one could see the rise of the landscape on both sides of the brown-water Douve River. On the St. Come du Mont, or northwest, side of the lock was a small twelve-foot by twelve-foot concrete service building that housed equipment and parts for the lock. On the Carentan side, or the southeast bank, stood the granite, concrete and timber two-story thatched-roof house that belonged to the lockkeeper. Several poplar and scrub trees decorated the land around the house. Separated from the house by some fifty feet was an old stone and timber barn. Road access from the east side was via a winding dirt road atop a dike, circling back and forth to the main highway. The lock was too narrow for vehicle traffic. Small carts and foot traffic were about the only ways to traverse the lock. Road access from the east was a rough dirt road that dropped from gentle hills around St. Come-Du-Mont, several thousand yards west.

From air reconnaissance photographs, Johnson had studied the problem thoroughly. Any force attacking the lock would have to cross wide stretches of open grassland, either on the narrow roadway or over land. Shallow ditches offered the only cover and concealment, and they were alongside the raised roadbed. It was certain that the Germans would have those roadways bracketed in the firing mission plans for their artillery on the hills near Carentan. A cross-country attack over the flat grasslands in broad daylight would be suicide. Anyone watching could see a thousand yards in all directions. Taking the lock under the cover of darkness was the best and obvious solution. Strike fast, strike in the night, and hold the position.

Two thousand yards northeast of the lock, two bridges crossed the Douve River. These were also part of the 501st objectives. Both bridges were sturdy enough for vehicle traffic and had to be under Allied control before the landing forces attacked the beaches. Another highway bridge and a railroad bridge crossed the Douve south of the lock and were included in Colonel Johnson's initial assault plan. One opinion was that the Germans would blow the bridges to keep Allied troops from Carentan. In that event, American forces would have to build temporary bridges to proceed, a time-consuming process that would hinder advancement towards Carentan.

Colonel Johnson placed complete trust in his officer corps. They were a well-disciplined leadership group. Training for the Normandy invasion had started months earlier in England. The tactical plan for each element of the airborne invasion was rehearsed over and over, down to the last and smallest detail. Night drops were a risk. Vision would be limited, landing areas may be obscured, and German forces would be at an advantage in having fortified positions. The paratroopers would have the element of surprise on their side. Johnson knew preparation was the most important factor. His men would be ready.

In any daylight drop, each stick could readily see and group up with their unit on the ground. Night drops were to be another matter to organize. Plans called for a simple procedure. Sims remembered, "Upon landing on the ground, the first man to jump would proceed in the same direction as the flight path of the plane, or towards the nose direction of the plane in flight. The last man to jump would walk towards the direction from which the plane had come, towards the tail section of the plane in flight. Those in the middle would sit tight until the others arrived. This was called rolling up the stick. Theoretically, they would meet somewhere in between, then form up into squads, platoons, companies, and battalions to advance on their objectives."

Allied commanders took another precaution. German air defenses were formidable, and it was known that some planes would fall victim to antiaircraft or machine gun fire. To minimize the chance that a regiment could be without leadership personnel if the commander's aircraft was shot down, the decision was made to divide regimental management staff into teams. Three full command teams were made up from the regimental staff officers. No two teams could be on any one aircraft. This procedure ensured that leadership on the ground would contain officers with intimate knowledge of all regimental and divisional objectives. Line officers were advised how this potential leadership structure would change if the regimental command staff did not survive the night flight.

Battalions had their own identity signals for reassembly on night drops. Some had audible sounds, like a bugle, that was to be blown to gather the paratroopers to one site to regroup. Another used a large bell to toll the signal. Some used a specific colored light to identify the gathering point. Others had helmet markings, like a small diamond or oval, which would be more visible as identification. Passwords and countersigns were issued to challenge an unknown figure in the dark. In addition, there was the "cricket," a small and oblong metal dime store noisemaker that made a distinct "click" when pushed in, and a "clack" when released. Each man had been issued the cricket before taking off from England. Upon meeting someone in the darkness, a paratrooper was to challenge by clicking the cricket once, for a sound of "click-clack." The proper response for identification was two clicks in return.

With the battalions in the 501st assigned to specific targets for the invasion, Colonel Johnson had repeatedly gone over each assignment with the unit commanders on models. Sims recalled them, "Sand table models were constructed to be as close to the actual terrain as was possible, using air reconnaissance photographs as their reference for accuracy. Undulations in the model were as close as possible to those of the proposed landing sites. Houses and villages, as well as roads, hedgerows, waterways and farms were recreated in a lot of detail. Even German gun emplacements, if recognizable from the pictures, were built into those models." Unit commanders then took their own individual platoon commanders over the sand table models to rehearse the plan. Platoon commanders took their platoons through the table model scenario so all could understand and see the relationship between their objective and those of other units. All preparations were made to add to the information, which would minimize problems that the lack of visibility caused during a night drop.

The 1st Battalion, under Colonel Johnson, was assigned the job of seizing and holding the la Barquette lock. The 2nd Battalion, under Lt. Col. Robert A. Ballard, was to blow up the Douve River bridges on the St. Come-Du-Mont to Carentan highway, and to capture St. Come-Du-Mont, as well as to destroy a railroad bridge crossing the Douve. Johnson would hold the 3rd Battalion in reserve. With those objectives accomplished, the regiment would control a southern line that included the flat lowlands between Carentan and St. Come-Du-Mont. Any German counterattack would be held in check along that line. The paratroopers would link up with the 4th Infantry coming inland from Omaha Beach. The combined units would then move forward to take Carentan and St. Lo.

First was the initial taking of the la Barquette lock and the bridges. That phase was the key ingredient. Rehearsals had gone smoothly. Johnson felt secure with the plan. His 501st only had to execute their part of the plan.

THE GROUND ARRIVES

"Childhood is the kingdom where nobody dies."
- Edna St. Vincent Millay

Lt. Hugo Sims positioned himself to avoid landing in the ink-black water. The sound of machine gun fire and the sight of tracers peppered the sky from multiple locations. Random paths of tracers streaked past as he continued the descent, but none followed his path towards the ground. The wind was in his favor. Turning his back to the wind helped him slip-drift past the water and land on soft and spongy, but reasonably dry land. Sims didn't have time to congratulate himself on avoiding the water. "I had to get the harness off. Then I flipped the mussette bag over my head onto my back. I left my unassembled carbine in the bag at first."

Planes droned in the air above, dipping and turning to dodge the anti-aircraft barrage and drop more paratroopers and Sims looked up, "One C-47 burst into flames and crashed to the ground, about 200 yards away, then burst with a violent explosion. I knew there would be no survivors. I did not see any other paratroopers nearby."

Sims had landed in the lowland marshy area between St. Marie-Du-Mont and the Douve River, southeast of Pouppeville. He had missed his drop zone by miles. The entire lowland area was crisscrossed with canals, ditches and grass that reached higher than his knees. Sims recalled the landscape, "There were shallow ponds and several high plots of land with trees. I could see dark outlines of farmhouses in the flatland. No lights shone at the houses, especially at this hour. French residents knew that any show of lights could be a magnet for machine gun and rifle fire from either side."

Sims did not know where he was. He knew that if he had missed the drop zone, so had most of his stick. Since he was the last man out of the plane, and the airspeed had been faster than it should have been, he knew the entire stick had to be spread over a wide area. Sims frowned, "I knew it would be nearly impossible to locate Major Allen. He had been the first out the door." Miles, not yards, probably separated the two paratroopers. He could only guess at where the balance of the regimental sticks had dropped. He remembered, "At that time it really didn't matter. I was alone and needed to orient myself and get moving."

Walking bent at the waist with all the stealth he could gather, Sims headed towards a subdued tree line, visible as a dark and foreboding clump in the faint moonlight. He recalled his next steps, "I stepped into a small canal and sank to my chin. I took a deep gulp of air and held my breath until I was sure I wouldn't go underwater. My two .45 pistols were in holsters and my carbine, still in the bag, was unassembled." Sims chose to assemble the rifle later in a more secure environment. The pistols were not military issue, but owned by Sims. "They were both mine. I had purchased them before I left the states." He cautiously continued towards the trees. "I crossed several more canals nearly covering my head again with water but each time I repeated the breath holding and continued." As he finally neared the trees he crouched lower to keep a small profile while he crept along silently.

"Some five minutes later," Sims recalled, "I heard a muffled sound like leaves rustling against trouser legs. I froze. I had one .45 pistol in my hand. Something was there in the darkness." Sims tensed. Easing his .45 up, he crouched lower, eyes straining to see in the darkness. Cautiously and very slowly, "I took the cricket in my other hand and gave the initial one click challenge." No response came.

Sims looked towards the ceiling and continued softly, "I eased back the hammer and cocked the pistol. I didn't know what was out there." His thoughts raced, heart surged faster. He held his breath. Another 'swish' sound was barely audible. He continued, "Whatever was there moved again." He stared to one side of the subdued sound of movement in the night, knowing his night vision would perceive movement better that way. "I tried the cricket challenge again thinking that I would shoot first if the proper response didn't come back." No response again. Whoever, or whatever, was out there was very close. "I could make out a faint shadow in the darkness. It was strange, but I didn't feel afraid." He had never been in combat, so how could he know how he would react. He felt tense more than fearful.

Sims spoke again, this time in lower tones, "I raised the cocked pistol, and aimed directly at the shadow, which was less than twenty feet away. I decided to wait until the last second before firing. That way I could shoot as many Germans as possible before they got me." Slowly and with a steady pull with his trigger finger, Sims took up the trigger slack. A split second before the .45 fired, Sims recognized the figure. It was another lieutenant from his stick. Exhaling in relief, Sims eased the hammer back down on his pistol and called out in a whisper to him. Sims smiled as he remembered, "A friendly English speaking voice responded."

The noise had come from a lieutenant from Sims' unit. "Thinking back, I never asked why he did not answer my cricket challenge. We were too glad to see each other in the night." Machine gun fire pierced the darkness, again streaking the air above ground with tracers of broken dotted lines of yellow, white and red in the night sky. Neither Sims nor the other man knew where any other members of their stick were. For that matter, Sims smiled as he recalled, "Neither of us knew where we were." Their conversation was whispered. Germans may have been within earshot. "We agreed we were way off the drop zone, which put us further away from our regimental objectives."

Sims had devised a plan. "The objectives for the 501st were the bridges over the Douve River and the La Barquette lock. My plan was to proceed southeast, towards the objective. I knew the importance of the lock in the overall plan. Colonel Johnson had stressed that many times back in England to everybody. I knew that the 501st must be scattered and I had no radio to contact any other unit, so I had to assume other units would also continue towards the objective."

Sims was adamant about one thing, "I felt the smartest course of action was to avoid contact with Germans. We could travel faster if we did not have to stop and fight through German positions." If they purposely sought out Germans and fought to the lock, sounds of those firefights would disclose their location and direction of travel. Sims decided that stealth was the best ally, at least until they could locate other paratroopers or reach the lock. This would also allow the element of surprise to remain on their side when approaching the lock.

Sims led off in the dark. The odor of decaying soil and dank stagnant water hung low over the ground. The odor of smoke from crashing planes joined the distinct acrid odor of cordite. Sims remembered that dark night walk, "Small shrapnel fragments continued to drop from the sky. Another five minutes passed as we proceeded towards the objective. Suddenly, we came upon another paratrooper who joined us after we exchanged the cricket challenge." The cricket was getting a workout. They added two additional men within minutes. "Machine gun fire erupted off to our right again and we heard the sound of an American M-1 and several carbines. A firefight between the Germans and paratroopers was going on in the dark. I skirted left, to make our way around the machine gun nest. The Germans hadn't detected us yet, and I wanted to keep it that way."

Continuing south, Sims waded in and through more standing water, sometimes waist deep. "The landscape was flatter than I expected, but the canals and ditches slowed our progress a good bit. We picked up several more stragglers in the next fifteen minutes."

Sims and his small unit had been on the ground for an hour when a noise out front stopped the patrol. A medic from the 1st Battalion, Pvt. Albert Hutto, had parachuted into the same lowland marshy area. As Hutto told George Koskimaki in his book, *D-Day With The Screaming Eagles,* "I found myself with five other privates or PFC's. Without anyone to take command, and without maps, we decided to dig in for the night in what appeared to be a cluster of trees in the half-light, several hundred yards away. Our first obstacle was a wide creek. One man swam across with a jump rope, and with a man at each end, we started pulling ourselves across. It was over our heads in the center. Four had crossed and I was about to start when a noise in the rear brought the two of us to the ground. I was sure it was Germans, but tried my cricket. After a few tense moments another cricket answered mine. I got up and met Lt. Hugo Sims of the 2nd Battalion of our regiment. I told him there were six of us, all privates, and that we were headed to dig in for the night. He was headed for the regimental objective. He had a dozen or so men with him and we quickly added six more."

Sims told of the next event, "There were several jump-injured paratroopers in the group, which was by then about twenty men. I saw a farmhouse on a small, elevated piece of land nearby, surrounded by some trees and shrubbery. I went forward to check out the house, which was enclosed by a partial stone and wood fence." Finding no one there, he took the men inside the fenced courtyard and instructed them to clean and oil their rifles. Weapons that had been through mud and water needed attention if they were to be effective when they met the enemy. Sims ate the first of his chocolate bars, his first meal in France. The short meal and rest felt good.

Sounds of combat pulsed from his right, further southwest. Sims said, "Separate battles were in progress and the sounds rose and fell, coming from multiple directions." The volume of fire grew harsh and loud, then dwindled into sporadic shots. Mortars and heavy weapons fire rang out in the darkness and exploded in muted lights. "More fighting started farther away. The sounds were more muffled and subdued. I thought about joining in the fight with some of the nearby paratroopers, but decided the correct decision was to get to the objective. The troopers fighting were well trained and good." Those skirmishes and confrontations could well be the deciding factor to delay Germans from defending the lock and bridges. Sims wanted to hurry. Speed and surprise would be his key elements.

"After the rifle cleaning," Sims concluded, " I knew the wounded men could not keep up with the rest of us. They also needed more medical attention. I ordered Pvt. Hutto and another medic to set up an aid station at the farmhouse for the wounded and took the remaining paratroopers and left toward the south." The sky was turning gray in the east as Sims led off. "We waded through more water, at times up to our chests. After skirting another German machine gun position, we went up a shallow bank to dry land. The machine gun fire into the sky had pretty much stopped. There were no planes in the air by then." Instead, the sounds turned to more rifle fire, both German and American, as they faced off in separate battles in the dark shadows. Battles were taking place in and around small villages as well as near German strong points.

Behind them in the pre-dawn gray light, heavy artillery barrages from the Navy offshore began battering Utah beach, softening up the landing area for the assault of the 4th Infantry Division. The 4th was already aboard landing craft and nearing the beach. The thundering sound of the big guns exploded with a lower and more powerful "Whoommp," followed by explosions on shore when the six and eight inch rounds splattered Utah beach. Sims had no way of knowing what was taking place out on the beach. If the assault did not succeed, the entire 101st and 82nd Airborne would be cut off and on their own. He could not concern himself with that. His focus was paying attention to his own precarious situation. They would have to cross the flat lowlands of the delta-like area to reach the lock in daylight, a formidable task.

Sims now had over 20 men with him. As he moved out he collected twice that many, ending up with a force of nearly 70 men advancing to LaBarquette lock. He kept a steady pace towards the south. They eased down into more water in the flat countryside. Wading was slow and tedious, but necessary. Sims spread the men out in a combat column, separating one from another by ten to fifteen yards for safety should an artillery round crash down on them. Fewer men would be killed or injured when they were spread out. In water up to his waist, Sims cautiously took one step at a time, ever watching for signs of German activity.

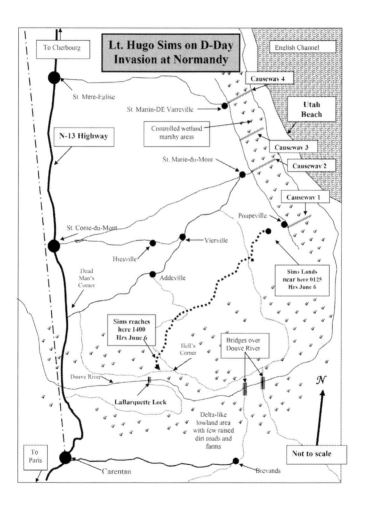

Lt. Hugo Sims on D-Day Invasion at Normandy

To Cherbourg

English Channel

Causeway 4

St. Mere-Eglise

St. Martin-DE Varreville

Utah Beach

Controlled wetland marshy areas

N-13 Highway

Causeway 3

Causeway 2

St. Marie-du-Mont

Causeway 1

Poupeville

St. Come-du-Mont

Vierville

Sims Lands near here 0125 Hrs June 6

Hiesville

Dead Man's Corner

Addeville

Sims reaches here 1400 Hrs June 6

Hell's Corner

Bridges over Douve River

Douve River

N

LaBarquette Lock

Delta-like lowland area with few raised dirt roads and farms

Not to scale

To Paris

Carentan

Brevands

37

Sims spoke, "As the morning wore on, we heard sounds of many more battles taking place off to our right, up in the hedgerows." He had no way of knowing that his own commander, Major Richard Allen, had landed on the proper drop zone and moved out towards the regimental objective.

In fact, Allen had landed within several hundred yards of the exact house he had targeted on the map for his jump. Allen later recalled the jump. "I landed right on target. I could see a house and some paratroopers nearby. I didn't even need to use my cricket to identify them. I gathered those men, about six or eight of them, and went to the house. All the lights were off and I knocked on the door. A Frenchman answered the door. I had studied foreign languages in school and could speak French, I asked him if I could come inside. I needed to lay out my maps and check our position to be sure of where I was. Inside, I could switch on the flashlight and review the maps." Allen smiled at the recollection, "The Frenchman was nice and told me to come in and then he spoke sternly, 'but first wipe your feet'."

Allen encountered German defenders in his trek toward LaBarquette lock. While in route, he took and occupied Addeville, a tiny fifteen-house hamlet southeast of St. Marie-Du-Mont. He had one hundred men to hold Addeville. The fight lasted throughout the darkness of the early morning hours and Allen found himself under German counterattacks as the sun rose. Allen had a problem. When Germans attacked there was no alternative but to stand and fight. If Allen left without engaging that force in Addeville, Germans there could counterattack LaBarquette lock in force. Allen had his hands full fighting at Addeville and advised Colonel Johnson in no uncertain terms that he could not break off and get to the lock. Johnson was in no mood to be left out near the open land at the lock and again sent word for Allen to break off the fight and come to the lock. Allen knew he couldn't comply and advised Johnson that he wasn't going to leave the fight at Addeville because the Germans may follow and attack his rear, which would only produce more fighting at a less favorable location. Johnson wasn't happy but he accepted Allen's answer, knowing that Allen would not disobey him without justifiable reason.

Colonel Johnson had had better luck than Sims in the jump. As Johnson prepared to jump, an equipment bundle got wedged in the door. No one could jump until the bundle was pushed out the door, causing a delay that placed Johnson right over his drop zone "D," southeast of Addeville and some two thousand yards from LaBarquette lock. He landed near his original drop zone, but had no radios. He sent several men out to locate the equipment bundles. Without radio contact with his battalion commanders he had no idea where they were or what their status was. Once he got a radio he still could not contact his battalion commanders because most of those commanders did not possess radios. Frustrated, but determined, he took off to LaBarquette lock himself. Arriving near the lock with a force of approximately 150 men, Johnson set up a command post in a farmhouse nearby. Using 100 of the men in a defense perimeter, he sent the remaining 50 to attack LaBarquette. He was surprised to find it lightly defended.

Surmising that the Germans would surely know that the lock was a major objective, Johnson was positive they would move to attack the lock at any moment. An attack would be imminent. Johnson was not going to chance losing control of the vital lock. He sent a small force to cross the lock and set up positions on the German side and proceeded to gather forces to strengthen his position.

Colonel Johnson had already reached LaBarquette lock by midmorning and wanted more men there to hold it against any potential German counter offensive. With Major Allen his operations officer, Johnson sent a runner to bring Allen and his forces to the lock. Communication was a disaster. With so many radios lost in the jump, or inoperable because they got soaked in water, most unit commanders resorted to the age-old method of sending runners between units to pass along information. Runners had to guess where to go to find another unit since they had no idea where those units may be located. It was a lengthy and frustrating task. Some runners encountered German forces and were killed or captured. Some unit commanders integrated runners into their units after receiving a message. Some runners didn't come back at all. There could be no coordination of effort in the battle where there was no communication.

Colonel Johnson did not know about the progress, or lack thereof, of his units near the beaches. Sand dunes separated the beach from the wet lowland between the beach and villages. Behind the sand dunes were four raised causeways acting as levies over which traffic could reach the small towns two miles inland. Those causeways were the only high ground the Allies could use in getting men and equipment inland after taking the beachhead. Tracked vehicles, like tanks and wheeled artillery, could not navigate the marshy lowlands between the causeways. They had to use the raised roadbeds on the causeways to get inland after crossing the beach and sand dunes. Johnson could only assume the causeway battle under the 506th was progressing as planned.

Colonel Ballard and his 2nd Battalion parachuted fifteen miles inland near St. Come-Du-Mont, his initial objective. Ballard was also one of the few who knew exactly where he was upon landing, having landed near his drop zone. Advancing on St Come-Du-Mont, Ballard found himself in a precarious position. He was on lower ground than the Germans and he had no artillery support. He decided he could not take the bridges or secure the village as in his operational plan until help arrived. He engaged in smaller battles during the hours before daylight.

Some German units were retreating from the villages north of Ballard's location. Ballard had those to contend with, and the road running south from Vierville intersected the main N-13 highway several thousand yards southeast of St. Come-Du-Mont, where more Germans had set up dug-in positions. Later, that intersection would become "dead man's corner," named as a result of a destroyed American tank with the tank commander's body still poised in the open turret, clearly visible from the waist up. He died in that position, his corpse charred from either the blast when the tank blew or the ensuing fire afterwards. He stayed there all day because the fighting was too vicious for anyone to remove the blackened and charred body.

Lt. Colonel Robert O. Carroll and his 1st Battalion had no chance to reach their objective. Landing in the hedgerows, Carroll was killed in a pre-dawn ambush at a crossroad, and most of the remaining elements of the 1st had been dropped so far away they wouldn't get back with the regiment for days. Some were dropped as far as seven miles south and southeast of Carentan, which was nearly three miles beyond the objective. Germans, well past forward elements of the Allies, captured some and killed others of those men. The 1st Battalion was spread so thin as to be almost a non-functional combat unit for the initial Normandy invasion. Some individuals who dropped nearer the correct drop zone were integrated into other units.

Colonel Johnson found himself with so little knowledge about his other units that he struck out to complete the regimental objectives, resigned that all he could do now was regroup his resources and get on with the plan. With Allen engaged at Addeville, Ballard up to his neck at St. Come-Du-Mont and Carroll missing, Johnson would take charge of the bridges and the lock. He had no alternatives; at least better communications were being established.

Lt. Hugo Sims had even less knowledge than Colonel Johnson about the situation. Both adjusted their thinking. Both knew little about success or failure of other units. Yet both appeared to hone in on the regimental objective from the start. Both had few men, little or no extra ammo, and few supplies from the pre-packed bundles that had been dropped before they jumped. Sims remembered, "I had even given my carbine to one paratrooper whose rifle was lost during the jump. A trooper with no weapon was no help in combat. I never saw the carbine again." Sims kept as weapons his two .45 pistols.

Sims had several miles remaining to reach the lock. By now it was broad daylight. Sunshine broke out between threatening gray clouds, then disappeared as quickly as it appeared. The scene was that of a marsh area with tall, thigh-high grass that approached waist high in places. Thick bushes and low trees dotted the landscape along the few roads across the lowland.

Sims recalled the surroundings; "Canals and ditches were more visible in the daytime. They had to be crossed. Barbed wire fences separated some of the farms. Cattle grazed in the grass pastureland. There were dead cows in the grasses, some having been hit by artillery or mortars, others by stray rifle and machine gun fire." Horses, some nervous and snorting, either grazed or with raised tail galloped off at the first sound of gunfire. Animals could not reconcile what was happening. All they could do was react. The shooting and explosions were as sudden and loud to them as it was to the paratroopers. The patrol kept to the original pathway southeast, spread out and in a combat-ready posture. "We were pretty exposed out in the open," Sims said. "I wanted to move out quickly."

Sims had been fortunate so far. He had neither been discovered nor had confronted any Germans. He had been on the ground since 1:45 in the morning. It was now mid-afternoon. He had been in the war for almost ten hours and hadn't fired a round. By that same time, there had been thousands killed or wounded in the fighting. His luck couldn't hold. Things would change, he was sure about that.

By 1500 hours, Sims could see the lock. It stood about eight feet above the grassland bridging a man-made dike on each side of the river. Sims saw men near the lock. Closer observation brought a relaxation in his breathing. They were American paratroopers. To avoid any misunderstanding and, perhaps being fired at by mistake, Sims proceeded in an orderly and observable procession toward the troops. Sporadic weapons fire continued to his right, up in the hedgerows again. Heavier artillery fire came from across the Douve, near Carentan. The raised causeway road, the N-13 from Cherbourg to Carentan, lay fifteen hundred yards beyond the lock from his present position. Waving to the paratroopers at LaBarquette, Sims recognized Major Allen, even at this distance. Sims and his patrol approached and reported in to Colonel Johnson. He then placed his seventy men under Johnson's command at the lock.

By the time Sims reached the LaBarquette lock, Colonel Johnson had radio contact with some units of the 501st. Though Johnson had requested Major Allen's presence at the lock most of the day, Allen was too engaged in the fight for Addeville. Only after he defeated the Germans at Addeville, leaving an aid station operating in the village, did Allen arrive at the lock with an assorted unit of men at about 1400 hours. Happy to see each other, Sims and Allen had time to relate what had happened after being separated on the jump. Sims smiled at the memory, "I sure was glad to see Allen. At least he had survived the night."

Sims discovered that, as he had suspected, Major Allen had come down in the hedgerows. Having been the first out of the plane, Allen had only met up with several others and proceeded toward the regimental objective at the bridges and LaBarquette lock. Not a part of his objective, Addeville became his biggest obstacle and had kept him occupied all of the night and past noon that day before he could disengage and move towards the lock. His descriptions confirmed Sims' suspicions that Sims had parachuted well past the drop zone.

Colonel Johnson set up an organized defensive perimeter around the lock. Night was coming and those defenses had to be in place and secure against a night counterattack. As Assistant G-3, Sims was assigned the task of locating and positioning foxholes for the FDL (Final Defensive Line) around the lock. "I set up firing lanes for machine guns and gave paratroopers in foxholes between the machine guns their firing lines. We had to dig in to be ready for any counterattack." He smiled as he recalled, "I dug the foxhole that Richard Allen and I would use." Mortars and small artillery fire were heard during the early evening and on into the night. Some random rounds landed in their area. Though none were killed, several men were injured in the attacks. Sims finally ate dinner on D-Day, another of his collection of chocolate bars. The sky was cloudy and overcast again. Rain arrived in small but annoying showers for several hours. By midnight the rain stopped and twinkling stars appeared overhead.

Before Colonel Johnson had secured the lock earlier in the day, there had been bitter fighting just north of the locks, at a tiny crossroad. Colonel Johnson had set up the CP there at a farm house after losing several men in a firefight at what became known as Hell's Corner. The Germans had bracketed that location for artillery and mortar fire before Johnson arrived and ambushed Johnson's men as they approached. Captain Sammie Homan was in on this action and told George Koskimaki, in *D-Day With The Screaming Eagles*, "We moved with Colonel Johnson to the locks. Most of the firing on us en route was from positions on high ground and relatively inaccurate. There was no cover or concealment so we felt like we were walking in front of targets on a known distance range." Johnson's mixed-unit of paratroopers succeeded in overrunning and holding the position.

During the early evening at dusk on June 6, Colonel Johnson sent a patrol to the two-targeted bridges upstream they were to destroy. They met stiff German resistance that sent up flares lighting up the area as in full daylight. Machine gun fire and mortars hit nearby. In short order the patrol returned, reporting the bridges too heavily defended to take with such a small force. Johnson would have to deal with that later, perhaps with a night attack. Mortar fire came in on the lock from the raised highway N-13, exploding around the lock, wounding more men. The highway was too far away for rifle or machine guns to retaliate with any accuracy. Paratroopers at the lock could only cringe and stay low in their foxholes until the barrage was over. The night would see even more mortar and artillery fire.

During the night, the paratroopers were able to get badly needed sleep between mortar and sporadic machine gun fire from across the river. By that time, they had not slept for two days. Sleeping would not be difficult, even with heavy weapons blasting away from across the Douve. Paired up in foxholes, they could sleep in shifts, one on guard while the other slept. A constant vigil was in order. Johnson sent out patrols during the night, more to keep alert to any German build-up across the lock than an offensive patrol action. They had accomplished much in those early hours of the invasion. There remained several obstacles to be overcome, but Johnson and his reduced corps of men still felt up to the job. At the conclusion of D-Day, the 501st was slowly regrouping at the inland command posts and assembly areas.

The scattered drops of the paratroopers may have caused confusion and problems for the Allies, but upon reflection, those very factors helped more than anyone imagined possible. The German war machine had vast experience and success in combat when they faced off in the traditional manner of using concentrated lines of combat with men attacking or defending one front. In such concentrations, reinforcements, advances and counterattacks can be somewhat predictable, at least in methodology. An enemy had distinct lines of battle. One side could advance or retreat from those lines.

Armies measured success or failure by movement of geographical lines. Reinforcements came from one direction, artillery was at a prescribed location behind one's own lines, and combat action was deployed at specific points to advance. The Germans were experts at flanking maneuvers and rigid fire discipline. Normandy was something else altogether. No distinct front lines, enemy in all compass directions, and reinforcements scattered and unorganized posed severe problems for the Germans. None of those factors fitted the German style of experienced combatants.

In the mass confusion of the turmoil created by missed drop zones and wide spread locations of paratroopers, German defenders faced an invading force that appeared to be attacking from every direction. No matter where or how the Germans tried to defend, or in which direction the Germans attempted a counterattack, the enemy appeared from somewhere else. They had no way of knowing where to secure reinforcements or where to send them. Each German force appeared to be surrounded by attackers. It looked to them like the main attack force had brought in the entire invasion force by air and dropped them all over Normandy and God knows where else. Communication lines were cut over vast areas. Germans could not communicate with their own forces. At first the scattered drops of the paratroopers appeared to be a liability, but Allied mistakes in the airborne invasion turned out to be an asset in defeating the Germans during those critical first 24 hours.

While some military analysts have countered that many of the defending German forces were made up of less experienced combatants and weaker German soldiers, it can be argued that even the well-oiled German elite units, some of which were involved in the battles at Normandy, would have encountered the same confusion as did the German defenders. No central attack line appeared to surface throughout the night, at least from a German perspective. Any retaliatory action the German forces took appeared to fail. It is not unreasonable to project that any combat unit, given identical circumstances, would have fallen upon hard times in deciding a course of action that would have succeeded in repelling the night invasion by the paratroopers.

There is debate even today, some 60 years later, of what may or may not have happened if the parachute drops had gone as planned. Those debates are theory and will never be resolved. The result became history. The 82nd and 101st Airborne, as well as the British 6th paratroopers scored dramatic victories. The first night drop in leading a major invasion had signaled a new day in the order of battle for future invasions.

The night of June 6 was only a start. Much remained for the paratroopers. Hard fought battles faced them in the coming hours and days. Lt. Hugo Sims had survived the most hellish night of his life, a night that saw many of his fellow 101st Airborne Division die in combat. There was little reason to rejoice when so many would not return. Rain drifted in during that first night at the lock, a drizzle rain that came and went during the dark, somber and foreboding, rain that caused men to think and reflect.

On June 7, the day following the beachhead landings, some battles were decided, while others were in question. The N-13 highway bridge between Carentan and St. Come-Du-Mont was still in German hands, as was the railroad bridge. LaBarquette lock was under American control, but was not entirely secure. St. Come-Du-Mont was being contested, but Colonel Ballard's Second battalion kept the Germans from attacking the lock. German troops would mount several counterattacks against St. Come-Du-Mont during that second day. Colonel Johnson had secured the southern line along the Douve River and dispersed his men around the lock to defend against any German offensive to recapture the lock. The two wooden bridges two miles north of the lock towards the beaches were in American hands. A defendable line from north to south across the lowland flood plain was steadily growing stronger.

The 4th Infantry Division successfully advanced across Utah Beach and met the paratroopers from 3rd Battalion of the 501st after crossing the southeastern causeway from Utah Beach at Pouppeville. The Americans had secured the three northwestern causeways earlier, and American units were advancing inland.

The beachhead landing at Utah beach took casualties, but far below expectations. The German defenders at Utah had been overwhelmed and overrun. Equipment and supplies to support the advancing 4th Infantry were being offloaded on the beach.

Progress in the hedgerow fighting was improving after American reinforcements with 4th Infantry entered the fight. Ste. Mere-Eglise was not yet in American hands, nor were key roadway junctions to the northwest towards Cherbourg, the next main objective for the Allies. The paratroopers took valuable footholds and they held on tight. Air support, in the form of P-47 fighter planes and light bombers, could assist ground forces without fear of German fighter planes. Artillery forces that came ashore on Utah steadily set up firing missions in support of the advancing Army forces. Through air superiority and good intelligence, the Allies were poised to continue toward the inland objectives.

Air drops of food and ammunition for ground forces improved as early as the second day, June 7. Ground forces were able to communicate with each other to coordinate troop movement and clear weather held, an unknown factor just twenty-four hours earlier. Forecasted rains and cloudy weather failed to show. American tanks from Utah Beach moved forward into positions with the 101st and 82nd Airborne, adding fire superiority for the Allies.

For the most part, German forces in and around the neck of the Cotentin Peninsula of Normandy had been defeated, killed, scattered or had surrendered. Most had retreated back towards either Carentan or Cherbourg. Those retreating towards Cherbourg were unknowingly heading for another round of combat with the paratroopers and American infantry that would end in another German defeat. The German effort at Cherbourg was doomed to fail; only the Germans could not believe it at the time.

The adjoining beachhead landing at Omaha was not going as well. Casualties were vastly higher and progress was slow. British forces had not advanced inland as quickly as planned, causing worry to Allied commanders. High cliffs at Point-Du-Hoc gave American Rangers the greatest challenge they had ever faced. Most of the Rangers died in the assault, but those remaining took out the German positions on the top. German forces had elevation in their favor on top of the cliffs and had fortified them with concrete and steel reinforced walls, sometimes as thick as four feet. Allied bombardment against those bunkers had not destroyed them as Allied command had hoped, which made the battle of the Rangers even more tenacious.

Still, the Normandy Invasion was a resounding success. German leaders and beach defenders had been caught by surprise. Hitler's forces were being defeated at each turn, though sometimes at a high cost. American and British paratroopers had been the spearhead of the invasion. That fact alone elevated the value and credibility of airborne effectiveness as a combat unit. There was still much to accomplish before the liberation of France could be labeled a triumph. Yet, the first two days dictated the tone of what would follow on the battlefields.

The original plan called for the airborne units to be pulled out of the battle after seventy-two hours. It was believed that their services could be utilized somewhere else in the war by then. In fact, the paratroopers had acted and performed as regular infantry units on the front lines after landing in the night. Their successes in the capacity of a combat front line unit met with such high praise that airborne units continued to lead the attack far longer than planned.

Hugo Sims had no time to relax. As Regimental Assistant G-3, his chief job function was in operations. He was to ensure that his commanding officer's battle plan and strategy proceeded as ordered. Sims shared a foxhole at LaBarquette with Major Allen. Word had passed down that the 4th Infantry had won the battle of Utah Beach. Sims and Allen felt more at ease with that news. At least they weren't stranded and cut off behind enemy lines. They had not linked up with the 4th, but they knew a reunion with Allied ground forces was near.

Patrols were sent out throughout the night, more to ensure security from a surprise counterattack by the Germans than anything else. Mortars arrived sporadically, as did the occasional artillery round. A tense night ensued. Dawn of June 7, D+1, would bring more troubles, troubles Sims knew would be challenging.

Sunrise over the delta on June 7 was an orange sphere with rainclouds threatening the eastern horizon as the paratroopers at LaBarquette lock awakened. Sims checked the foxholes surrounding the lock to be sure paratroopers were awake and alert. He had been up for two hours, scanning the surrounding lowlands as the sky went from black to gray, then on to sunrise. Attacks often came at those early hours, as history showed that those times were the most favorable for attacks. The enemy was thought to be at low alert just before daylight, sleepiness lingering after a night of standing watch. Satisfied that all was in order, Sims returned to the foxhole he shared with Major Allen.

Germans still controlled the highway bridges, as well as the railroad bridge over the Douve a thousand yards south of their position. Both bridges were yet to be captured by the 501st. After all, that was part of the original plan. The one-day delay did not change that assignment. Colonel Johnson was devising the new plan of attack. Several engineers had dropped with the 101st and 82nd, as well as demolition experts with their explosives. If the bridges could not be captured and controlled, then Johnson was going to blow them. If the Americans couldn't use them, neither would the Germans.

June 7 was a Wednesday. It would not be a typical Wednesday, nor would it bring a quiet summer day. Instead, Wednesday would prove to set important wheels in motion for the 501st. Hugo Sims arrived at LaBarquette still a rookie, at least in the sense he had not faced off in a toe-to-toe battle with German forces. His parachute jump into a strange country presented him with a new set of challenges in his young life, but the horror of the night drop and seeing planes spiral to the ground in resounding crashes amid the hectic defenses of the German forces had given him a small window to view what was ahead. That window was not fully open yet.

Colonel Johnson was in a dither because he had not accomplished all his objectives on the 6th. Now in control of the lock, he meant to move on and take the highway bridges and the railroad bridge on N-13. June 7th arrived under more heavy artillery fire from German forces across the Douve, and mortars continued to explode around and in their position at the lock. All morning the men defending the lock came under sniper fire. Walking upright was an invitation for the Germans to open fire.

Johnson scheduled a re-supply plane to make a drop of ammunition and supplies at 0630 that morning. Precisely on time, the planes arrived and dropped their bundles of supplies, but none were near enough to the lock for Johnson's men to retrieve them, nearly a mile distant in the swampy grasslands to the north. With two hundred and fifty men, ammunition became Johnson's most critical need. His paratroopers couldn't fight without ammo.

The sun remained bright and clear all morning. Sounds from nearby battles rumbled across the lowland valley. German and Allied artillery rounds screeched across the sky. Allied fighter planes and light bombers zipped through the air, in route to targets of opportunity throughout the area. Men were exhausted from their baptism by fire in combat. Some had time to catch a few winks while others stood watch. The paratroopers were calm, going about their assignments like experienced veterans. Some ate K-rations. Hugo Sims stayed with chocolate bars. Weapons needed cleaning and foxholes needed work to bolster against the attack Johnson felt was sure to come. By midmorning, Johnson and his group gave up on moving toward the bridges and decided to hold the lock since the supply drop had failed. There was not enough ammunition to do both.

Nearing 1500 hours on June 7th, a large troop movement was spotted approaching from the north, heading toward LaBarquette lock from the direction of Utah Beach. Even with binoculars Johnson could not tell if the forces were Allied or German. The formation came across the grasslands almost in rag-tag groups clustered together as they walked, not at all like a military force in a combat zone. Johnson passed the order for the men around the lock to stay low. As the soldiers approached to within a thousand yards Johnson studied them through the glasses.

As Major Allen recalled, "We could see them clearly, but it was difficult to identify who they were at such a distance. As they came a little closer we could see they were German paratroopers. The German paratrooper helmet was molded differently around the ear from their normal infantry helmets."

If they continued on their present heading the entire force would walk right into the paratroopers' position. Johnson quickly devised a course of action. Assembling several officers, Sims and Allen among them, Johnson gave the men his directives. The paratroopers would stay in their foxholes, out of sight to the approaching Germans. No one was to fire a weapon until the machine gun on the right flank opened fire. Johnson would be near that position and would personally order the machine gunner to fire.

Sims and several other officers crawled from one muddy foxhole to another to give strict orders as to when they were to open fire. Not one round was to go off until that machine gun fired. Each officer crept low, well below the vision of the oncoming Germans. Sims cautioned each man again about staying low and holding fire until the signal came and then returned to his foxhole with Major Allen.

Johnson's men had dug their foxholes in a rough "U" shape on the St. Come Du-Mont side of the lock, the open end of the "U" facing the approaching Germans. The open end of the "U" was splayed out so that no paratrooper on one side would be firing towards a paratrooper on the opposite side of the "U." Each man assembled his ammo where he could reach it quickly. There were six machine gunners who quickly moved low to the ground, shifting positions to face the Germans. The gunners laid in a fresh ammo belt and snapped the bolt back, letting it chamber a round. Silently they watched the Germans continue slowly, unaware of the paratrooper's presence ahead. Sims waited like the others, anxious but confidant. Surprise was on their side.

The entire German element was now in full view. Johnson realized his unit at the lock was far outnumbered. He estimated the number of Germans to be nearly 500 men, at least twice his number of men. The paratroopers must be effective with their accuracy and they would need to start the ambush when the Germans were far enough away to keep them from rushing Johnson's position. The superiority of German numbers could cause a real problem if the paratroopers waited until the Germans were too close to start the ambush. Above all, the paratroopers would have to maintain rigid fire discipline and hold their concealed positions.

The Germans walked almost nonchalantly, obviously thinking there were no Allied forces anywhere near. Front elements of the German procession were walking casually, not holding their firearms at the ready position. Some carried rifles on their shoulders, hands gripping the barrel facing forward and pointed at the ground. The remainder of the German unit appeared to be equally as unconcerned about their surroundings. Men were walking in small groups and spread out in small clusters, talking with others while they continued toward the lock. The distance closed to five hundred yards. Johnson and his force watched in silence. Time crept slowly for the waiting paratroopers.

At 1600 hours, the forward elements were 350 yards out in front of the American troops. This distance put them squarely in range of the guns of the paratroopers.

Johnson would wait no longer. He couldn't risk being seen or discovered. The element of surprise would be gone. Looking one last time to properly verify the distance, Johnson gave the machine gunner the order, "OK, now. Let'em have it!"

Only a fraction of a second passed after the first machine gun fired until the entire paratrooper unit opened up in a storm of rifle and machine gun fire. Bullets tore into the approaching Germans, tossing some to the ground dead and wounding others as those troops scurried to respond. They had, indeed, been caught by surprise. A fierce firefight ensued, lasting nearly thirty minutes. Bullets ripped into both sides in the fight. Dirt splattered from rounds hitting too low to hit fighters on each side.

The German commander called for artillery and mortar support from German forces near St. Come Du-Mont. In minutes those rounds crashed into the paratrooper's position in loud and earth splattering explosions. Clods of earth exploded upward. Shrapnel zinged through the air. No time to talk. Paratroopers clenched their teeth unconsciously as they methodically fired round after round. The paratroopers' first volley took out the lead elements, then moved deeper into the German force.

Germans dove to the ground and returned fire. They were scattered and unable to regroup to mount a counterattack. They were caught in open territory. Bullets zipped into the earth around them, slicing and cutting the tall grass in the process. From his position in the foxhole with Major Allen, Sims joined in the fight, his first time firing at Germans since he arrived. He leveled an M-1 he had acquired after reaching the lock and fired slowly and deliberately, squeezing the trigger instead of pulling it on each round. He saw his first target slump to the ground. Sims found himself strangely calm, focusing on the job at hand, but alert. Training was paying off. Tall grass concealed the Germans as they dove or fell to the ground.

Sims spoke quietly, "There was no way to know how many Germans were killed. Wounded cried out in the firefight. We kept firing into the Germans for about 30 minutes."

Return fire from the Germans subsided, tapering off to a few sporadic pulses. Paratrooper firing also mellowed. Few targets were visible. Colonel Johnson determined it was time to make an offer for the Germans to surrender. Most of the Germans were pinned down in the open and there was no escape. Johnson's men were running low on ammunition and he didn't want to fire it all until he could get either more manpower or additional ammunition. Johnson's paratroopers wanted to fight it out until every last German was dead. Johnson would have none of that.

Johnson sent word and asked for volunteers to accompany him out to offer the surrender. Getting several to step forward, Johnson ordered the other paratroopers to cease firing. The small group, one a German-speaking interpreter, walked forward under an orange flag lifted on a rifle. Orange was the color Allied High Command had selected to designate friendly forces. Major Allen and Sims followed. Every unit in the invasion carried orange banners for identity purposes. Sims recalled, "Allen and I followed by about fifty yards. I remember a PFC, I think his name was Runge or something like that, and he was right beside Johnson. He spoke fluent German and was going to act as interpreter for Johnson." The Germans ceased firing from the grassland, but mortar and artillery fire from Carentan and St. Come Du-Mont continued.

Sims recalled, "Colonel Johnson neared the closest Germans when we heard rifle fire coming from our own men behind us. We weren't sure if all the men had gotten the word to cease-fire or whether they just didn't obey. Johnson and the rest of us continued another 50 yards. All firing stopped by then."

Sims breathed deeply, "Then the Colonel went another twenty-five or thirty yards and several Germans stood up. The standing Germans hit the ground and firing started from the German lines. All of us hit the ground together, hugging the dirt, faces in the grass." Paratroopers on the American line saw the action and started a flurry of rifle fire at the Germans. Johnson and the men wiggled and belly-crawled back to the paratrooper lines, although as Sims recalled, "Not before one man was shot in the arm and Colonel Johnson had been hit in the hand." Firing continued for another thirty minutes or so. Artillery and mortar rounds came in again.

Johnson wasn't ready to give up on offering the Germans a chance to surrender without being destroyed. He again ordered his men to cease-fire. The volume of German fire subsided. Johnson and the same men walked out towards the swamp again. Sims recalled, "Two Germans took slow steps toward Johnson, unarmed. The two Germans said they wanted to surrender but their commanding officer had already killed several other Germans for talking about surrender. The Colonel sent them back to their own line with the ultimatum that the Germans had thirty minutes to surrender, or in Johnson's words his men would 'annihilate you – to the last man'. The Germans returned to their lines and we went back to our lines."

Firing erupted again, by both sides. Another thirty minutes passed. German fire slowed, then abruptly stopped. Sims recalled the next events, "Colonel Johnson ordered that all our men hold their fire if Germans stood up and walked unarmed toward our lines. A few Germans rose and headed for us, unarmed. At first, the Germans came forward one or two at a time then larger groups joined them. Within minutes most of the entire German force surrendered."

Suspicious paratroopers held their fire but remained alert to any possible move that might signify a concealed assault instead of surrender. Each paratrooper kept his sights on a German as the process unfolded. The Germans were sincere. Surrender was their intent, and surrender they did.

Johnson discovered that the German unit was the experienced and veteran 6th Parachute Regiment, one of Hitler's best fighting units. After having been dropped in support of the beachhead defenses, they had become part of the German forces Colonel Ballard had fought earlier in the day near the beach causeway by Pouppeville. Final counts showed that 350 prisoners surrendered and 150 German soldiers were dead. More wounded Germans lay in the grassland. Johnson counted ten Americans killed and thirty wounded in the fight. Outnumbered by more than two-to-one, the paratroopers of the 501st had performed well above the expectations of their leader.

Major Allen and the other officers were puzzled. Allen recalled, "We couldn't understand why they were coming from the beach direction. It was obvious that the Germans defending the beaches needed help and this was an experienced combat unit. We never did discover why they were casually walking through the lowlands that day."

Sims now looked his enemy eye-to-eye. The Germans were not much different from him, except in their youth. Sims recalled, "Many appeared to be teenagers, some as young looking as fifteen. They all appeared tired and unkempt. Several of the officers had a belligerent attitude even as prisoners. Their uniforms were dirty and muddy." Most appeared to have resigned themselves to captivity, many believing it was far preferable to being killed by a determined-to-succeed enemy such as the 501st paratroopers. Still, Sims had a deep sense of satisfaction at having faced the enemy and not wavered.

The paratroopers under Colonel Johnson now had an additional task: guarding prisoners until someone could take charge of them and take them back behind Allied lines, which were not as clearly defined as the paratroopers had hoped they would be by that time. A small detachment of paratroopers was stationed around the group of prisoners, including an interrogation team. Information from the prisoners could clarify what the Allies fighting in the hedgerows were up against.

Inside the lockkeeper's house would be the interrogation point. At the precise moment one of the interrogation members, Captain Altus F. McReynolds, the regimental adjutant, approached a German officer, a German 88 artillery round came flashing through an open window squarely in the midst of the of the men inside. Twenty of the Germans and Captain McReynolds were killed in the blast. An American paratrooper was killed and Major Allen was narrowly missed as a second 88 exploded near the command post.

The second 88 wounded the regimental surgeon, Major Francis E. Carrel. Major Carrel dressed his own wound and continued to care for other wounded men. Hell's Corner was gaining a reputation for violent fighting filled with unseen dangers from a tenacious enemy nearby and across the Douve.

Sims and the acquired forces of paratroopers from other units were to stay at the lock for another night. Johnson wasn't ready to give up on his original targeted objectives, the railroad bridge and two highway bridges. They would have to wait another day. Perhaps the additional day would allow time to gather more forces for the job. Paratroopers were still arriving from points around the compass. If Johnson could gather more of the 2nd Battalion the job would go smoother. After all, the 2nd had been assigned the job in the first place. They would be more familiar with the plan than members of other units. If he could not gather in the 2nd Battalion, he would form an assault force from the paratroopers on hand and supplement them with men who may arrive over the next eight or ten hours.

Hugo Sims settled in for another night at the lock, sharing the foxhole dug for himself and Major Allen.

Sims recalled that night, "Germans fired mortars and artillery rounds all night, but we were so tired we slept pretty good under the stars."

Dirty, mud-caked and tired, Sims retained enough energy to rise and check the foxholes to ensure someone was awake and alert during the night. As G-3, he wasn't going to be surprised by a German night attack because someone was asleep when they should be on watch, nor did he want a German unit to probe their positions during the night and get away, which would allow Germans to register the exact location of the paratroopers at the lock and set up mortar and artillery attacks with greater accuracy. To avoid that, Sims knew the best defense was to have men who were alert and ready to react if something or someone moved in the dark outside their perimeter.

D+1 ended with a successful ambush, 350 prisoners, no ground given or lost to the Germans, the two bridges north of the lock secure in Allied hands, and American paratroopers and infantry units enjoying a firm foothold inland from Utah beach. Colonel Johnson still did not know about airborne losses. It was far too early to get accurate information about what had happened to many of the sticks. Assessment of any manpower factors would be a haphazard guess. He would stand pat with the information he had and use new data as it flowed in from dependable sources.

Support elements for the 501st started to arrive on June 7, but were more abundant by June 8. The 377th Parachute Artillery Battalion jumped with the 501st and lost 11 of their 12 howitzers on the drop. On D plus 2, the 377th got two 7.62 howitzers captured from the

Germans, taken by members of the 327th glider forces. The 65th Armored Field artillery Battalion had come ashore on D-Day (H plus 3 hours) and was attached to the 101st. This would be their main artillery for several days. More artillery and ammunition were being off-loaded at Utah and would be sent forward over the coming days. Ammunition grew steadily more available by D+2, and reinforcements started to trickle in to replace those lost in the initial night assault.

Colonel Johnson had reason to breathe a little easier. Close air support was a radio call away. Heavy artillery was close by. Antiaircraft machine guns had come ashore and could be placed in service under his command if needed.

Sims recalled that day, "Supplies started to arrive by D+2. Razor blades, razors, and shaving cream arrived. Red Cross personnel attached to the 101st delivered cigarettes and chewing tobacco, matches, and more towels for us."

June 8 saw the issue of St. Come-Du-Mont rise in the level of importance. That village represented one of the unsecured sectors of Johnson's assignment. The highway from St. Come-Du-Mont to Carentan, the N-13, was critical. If the highway remained under German control there was danger of counterattacks and severely limited space for Allied forces to advance south and east of the Douve towards Carentan. Capture and control of St. Come-Du-Mont meant control of that highway for the allies. It became clear that the 101st was going to have to take immediate control of the town in order to quickly open the highway route south. The capture of

St. Come-Du-Mont and the Douve crossings became increasingly urgent.

Colonel Robert F. Sink, 506th commander, was given the St. Come-Du-Mont task. He knew the area and had enough manpower resources to accomplish the job. Johnson had units nearby, but they were already engaged in other battles. Sink would undertake capturing St. Come-Du-Mont on the morning of June 8. The plan called for Sink to then move down the N-13 and secure the Vierville Road junction, Dead Man's Corner, above the flatlands just east of St. Come-Du-Mont. The battle would be hard fought. German positions were dug in and well defended. German machine guns and mortar support were plentiful, and the entire area was still in range of the heavier German 88s at Carentan.

Sink was up to the task. Though the battle lasted all day, sunset showed both St. Come-Du-Mont and Dead Man's Corner in American hands. The causeway east towards Carentan presented more challenges. The roadway was elevated, offering excellent cover and concealment for Germans to lay in ambush. Any attempt to move men and equipment down the N-13 would meet formidable resistance. There would be no easy fighting to take the highway.

Four bridges crossed the Douve and several tributaries between St. Come-Du-Mont and Carentan. The first two bridges presented Sink with less a challenge than the last two. Bridges 3 and 4 were closer to Carentan. The closer the Allies got to Carentan, which was fifteen miles inland, the further they were from their own support elements. Wheeled artillery and heavy weapons transported behind

Jeeps would not reach across the raised roadway. They were exposed and out in the open clearly visible to the enemy. German marksmen with artillery and mortars would pick them off as they attempted to drive down the roadway. One bridge, bridge 4, had been partially destroyed. No vehicles could pass over the bridge until engineers came forward and made necessary repairs. Sink would have to take the roadway without armored support.

Lt. Hugo Sims remained at LaBarquette lock with Colonel Johnson's forces. His task was the defense of that position. German counterattacks could swiftly flank any battle for the roadway if Johnson and his forces left their position at the LaBarquette lock to join the battle for St.Come-Du-Mont. Sims would spend the day listening to sounds of the fight. He followed the progress from radio reports, but the sounds of fighting moving down toward the causeway bridges gave proof that Colonel Sink was progressing. Mortars and artillery still exploded in their area, showering clumps of grass and dirt high into the air to rain back down on the men in their foxholes. They could not retaliate. Targets were out of range for the weapons they had at the lock. They could only sit it out and hope the shells exploded without death or injury to the paratroopers.

On the morning of June 10, Lt. Hugo Sims moved out from the lock to the small village of Vierville. The men who had fought for the lock had been relieved. At last, infantry units coming ashore on Utah Beach reached Colonel Johnson's position at the lock and took over the position. Sims and members of the 501st PIR would refit and prepare for their next action.

Vierville was situated less than two miles northeast of the lock, and the village had few accommodations, but they could sleep under a roof for a night or two. One crossroad passed through the small village and was filled with American soldiers. Some milled about reminiscing over the action from the past few days. Others were wounded, awaiting transport to other medical facilities. There were the usual bragging conversations, mixed in with comments and thoughts of paratroopers killed or missing in action.

"Anybody seen Larson?"

"Nah, not since we jumped."

"Where's the 502nd?"

"Man, you shoulda seen that Kraut when Jimmy charged with that Tommy gun."

"Whoever made these K-rats ought to be shot."

"The chocolate bars are like bricks."

"Peterson, you got any smokes?"

"I'd give three bucks for a cold Schlitz."

Men ate, some the first hot meal since arriving on French soil. Others nursed sore muscles and sprains left unattended while they battled the Germans at the lock. Laughter was heard at some joke or prank, the first sign men were bringing themselves back to normal. Smiles at seeing someone thought to be killed appeared when that man entered the area, followed by backslapping joy and more laughter.

While it was no time – and definitely not the place – for a party, the 501st was embracing the friendship of each other. Men in combat possess an unspoken but nonetheless special relationship with others who faced death and survived. Tough and battle seasoned now, the macho image was apparent in the set of the shoulders and the straight backs as paratroopers walked. They had met the Germans head-on and come out the victor. A degree of braggadocios was in order, maybe even some of the swagger, as paratroopers relaxed for a short time.

"Larimore, I thought the Krauts got you!"

"Nope. I got them first."

"Heard from Kenner?"

"Jackson said he got hit bad. Check with the medics."

"Got myself a Luger yesterday."

"Know when we're going to get a hot meal?"

"Couldn't tell you."

"Hey, Captain, we gonna be here long?"

"Don't know, Carson, but I doubt it."

Paratroopers mingled with artillery troops. Infantry sat beside glider pilots. Rivalries spanning decades were set aside. A sense of accomplishment and relief presided. They had survived. Each had faced unspoken fears and walked away. Many had not. American paratrooper bodies were strewn throughout the French countryside, undiscovered as yet. Bodies of dead German troops mixed with the rancid odor of dead horses and cattle in the hedgerows and fields.

The sight of all those dead bodies wore heavily. Torn and shattered almost beyond recognition as human remains, bodies lay in grotesque positions, some with blank eyes staring out into space, others with no head, some with arms and legs blown off. Bloody leg and arm stumps lay in the hot sun. Some dead facial expressions looked as though they died while sleeping with no wounds visible.

The mixture of American troops around the command post displayed varied emotions. Filthy and dirty faces showed tired and hollow eyes of the haunting Thousand Yard Stare. That look would grow in time to become a benchmark of men who survived horrid battles and the accompanying sights and sounds: men who walked into a nightmare beyond their worst imagination and returned. Parts of that nightmare would never go away.

Buildings in Vierville appeared bleak as the landscape; some torn and blasted to almost nothing but rubble, some half standing, and some looking like no war was anywhere near. Livestock that survived the initial battles ambled aimlessly down roads and through fields, some limping from injuries received during the fight. Dead horses and cows lay bloating in fields nearby, the stench growing by the hour. Trees had limbs blown off and the hedgerows had undergone dramatic changes when tanks and heavy artillery blasted away at them until they were destroyed to allow troops to pass through them instead of climbing over.

The Normandy landscape was taking on the look of a country at war, all right. It was visible in the faces of local citizens as well as the scenery. They were happy to have liberators show up, but a huge rebuilding and repairing project was in store for them. Downed fences and hedgerows meant livestock was scattered and missing. Those same locals lost friends and loved ones in the fighting even though they were unarmed and not a part of either fighting force. Funerals and new graves loomed in their immediate future. Who did the killing did not matter. Death was all around them: Americans, Germans and French. The sights and smells lingered long after the battles. It was still just the beginning.

But Carentan was waiting. The town of 65,000 people across the Douve was still in German hands. Carentan presented the next obstacle for the Allies. Before France could be crossed, Carentan lay directly in the path. It would be a troublesome task, filled with dangers Sims and the 501st hadn't seen yet, but they would have to take Carentan. Colonel Johnson received orders on June 10 to move out on the morning of June 12. He would have all three of his battalions for the job. While many paratroopers slept or refitted, Johnson and his staff officers were deep into the battle plan.

German command understood the importance of Carentan. The city represented the communication center of the entire Cotentin Peninsula. It was also the stepping-off point for any enemy troop movement towards Paris and points east toward Germany. Carentan was the first city of consequence east of the Douve, overlooking the entire delta. American forces must cross the open delta and narrow and targeted causeway from St. Come-Du-Mont before attacking the city. In such an action, a German foothold in Carentan would control those avenues of approach. Rommel was a worthy opponent for the Americans. His direct order for German defenders in Carentan contained the words to "defend Carentan to the last man, the last bullet." That left little room for misinterpretation. Rommel had experienced, battle hardened veterans poised for the battle. If the Americans did capture Carentan, Rommel had prepared a full counterattack plan to recapture the city.

On Sunday, June 11, the 501st moved out across the Douve, some two miles south of LaBarquette lock. Sims continued as the Assistant G-3 for Major Richard Allen, and had been over the plan thoroughly. Once on the eastern side of the river, Johnson gathered his regiment for a final briefing at Segueville, a crossroad village with several houses about four thousand yards east-northeast of Carentan, before jumping off in the attack. He had requested, and received, a tank complement to support his attack. He would also have the 327th Glider Infantry and several additional infantry units to help encircle the town.

Command of the Carentan operation would fall under General Anthony C. McAuliffe, the 101st Artillery commander who later would become famous for his Bastogne reply to a German request that Americans surrender. The 327th would attack from the east. The 502nd and 506th would attack from the west and south, across the just captured and cleared causeway from St. Come-Du-Mont to Carentan. The 327th Field Artillery battalion had crossed the Douve and set up near Catz, and would place heavy artillery barrages on Carentan. The plan called for surrounding the town, then capturing any Germans remaining in the encircled city. The 501st would be held in reserve.

The attack started at 2000 hours on June 11. It raged through the night, with strong German resistance at multiple compass points. The most rigid German positions were located northeast of Carentan, on Hill 30. That strategic hill overlooked much of Carentan and German heavy machine guns and light artillery were well dug in on the hill. The attack was slowing. Johnson called up the 501st the next morning. No longer in reserve, they would approach from the east, attacking under a barrage of smoke and covering artillery fire. The 2nd and 3rd Battalions attacked abreast of each other, with the 3rd Battalion on the right side alongside the Carentan-Isigny highway, the right hand boundary of the line of attack. The Canal de Vire-et-Taute was to be crossed in the attack.

Approaching the canal, it was discovered to have overflowed its banks, flooding most of the nearby valley. The flooding caused the entire frontal attack to be over land that was covered in water, far too deep in places to maintain a proper formation.

Sims recounted, "The canal was too deep to wade comfortably. We couldn't keep a straight attack line across our front. It seemed like the right or left side was always being bogged down in the water. Some places the water was up to our waist. That meant our ammo belts dragged in the water. It was a mess. It was difficult to stay on our feet with the slippery mud underneath. Somebody fell and cursed the water. It didn't take long for the CO to change tactics."

The full two battalions were forced to reduce to single file to cross the canal. They crossed a partially wrecked railroad bridge before continuing the attack. "The first company," Sims told, "I think it was Company H, had crossed the canal and was nearly across the open pastureland area when German mortars and artillery came in on us. Company H rushed Hill 30 and wiped out the machine gunners and most of the artillery positions."

"Company H continued the attack on Hill 30. Company I went into Carentan and turned around to attack the opposite face of the hill. Both companies were met by heavy German fire from a tracked vehicle. Our artillery continued to pound the position with white phosphorous rounds in an attempt to rout the Germans. As artillery rounds landed in and around the German positions, the Krauts slacked off. Companies H and I went ahead and completed the defeat of Hill 30." Sims finalized the scene, " The three-pronged attack worked pretty well and we didn't have any more problems with Germans up there."

The 101st, supported by artillery and tanks, rushed into Carentan. German artillery rounds shattered stone and mortar from buildings, spewing shards of concrete and glass into the air. Machine guns clattered from houses and fortified positions at strategic street intersections and dug-in fortifications. Each had to be taken. A German 88, cleverly concealed in the false front of a building, was destroyed. An anti tank armor unit took it out in three short but devastating rounds. Each street presented new places where the enemy could hide so small units took the initiative to destroy positions and kill Germans. Carentan was vicious fighting. Germans not killed or captured slowly retreated in the battle.

Rommel may have ordered the Germans to defend to the last man and last bullet, but he wasn't able to offer enough combat support to help them in the fight. Most German prisoners had little or no extra ammunition. Food was scarce among the prisoners and medical treatment from their own medical teams appeared to be almost non-existent. German tanks were in short supply for the Carentan battle, and no air support was visible. American P-47's had total air superiority. German soldiers had to feel somewhat abandoned by their superior officers in the absence of so many vital elements to a battle.

While sporadic battles continued to take place, some furiously contested, the city was in American hands before dark. The advancing 501st discovered abandoned German artillery and tanks, along with small arms and machine guns. Some door-to-door street fighting broke out near the rail yard but was swiftly won by the Allies. The German defense had not been nearly as fierce as Allied command anticipated.

While the battle for bridge number 4 coming in from St. Come-Du-Mont had been devastating to the 502nd, it was finally taken, followed by a frontal bayonet charge led by Colonel Robert Cole during the day across an open pasture to wipe out a German machine gun position. Cole won the Medal of Honor for that action, but he never received it. He was killed in Holland before having the medal pinned on his uniform.

By dark on June 12, the 101st had another combat success to their record. German forces continued to harass the Allied troops with weak counterattacks and random artillery barrages for another night. Street fighting had come to a close except for two or three small firefights from desperate German infantry forces attempting to carry out Rommel's orders. It was futile. The American forces were too powerful and too well supported. German occupation of Carentan was at an end.

Carentan was the final battle action for the 501st in the Normandy campaign. The regiment spent another three weeks in France, mainly as defenders of the ground around Carentan. There would continue to be German counterattacks, but their energy and effort was only a faint attempt to regain the city. Germany had lost Carentan for good. Those few counterattacks after June 13 were small unit actions doomed to fail from the onset.

Allied forces from the Omaha Beach and Utah Beach invasions linked up at Carentan, forming the tip of an Allied attack plan to traverse France. Caen and St. Lo were battles yet to be fought, but Sims and the 501st were not a part of those operations. Those battles would be completed by the end of July.

Sims and the 501st returned to a small village near the coast at Utah beach, just west of causeway 4. It was there they would depart Normandy. Donning their gear and equipment, the regiment walked down to the beach. On July 14, at 1400 hours, the 501st boarded LSTs (Landing Ship Transport) to return to England.

Sims recalled the trip back to England as, "The best ride we had so far. It didn't take too long and we watched France slip away over the stern of the LST. I sure was looking forward to a dry bed and a hot shower."

Normandy was his initial test, and Hugo Sims passed the exam. Whatever fears he harbored before he jumped into the French night sky were now neatly tucked away. When facing the reality of war, he did not succumb to failure. He stood firm at LaBarquette and faced elite German parachutists with a calm resolve to perform his duty. An inner calmness enters the mind when a soldier has found that knowledge. Sims would not begin to like war or the firefights and killing, neither then nor ever. Sims was awarded a Bronze Star for his actions in Normandy.

Watching friends and fellow paratroopers die dampened the victories. Never again would Hugo Sims speak to or see those faces. Those who died had done their part, and the part of someone else. As Sims said, "The heroes are still over there. They will be forever." But Sims would clutch the memory of them throughout his life. Normandy was behind the youthful lieutenant. The war still raged. A new battle was ahead, that much he knew. However, he now knew he was up to the task. What he didn't know was just how soon the next task would take him to a higher level, and that the coming mission would test his resolve with far greater risks.

The 501st returned to England after the Normandy campaign. They had left the old and worn England just over a month earlier, green and rambunctious young paratroopers looking for a fight. They returned to find a different England from the one they knew before Normandy. England had been at war for years. The English people had grown weary with the uncertainty of bombs dropping in the midst of evening tea or bedtime. There were solemn faces on Englishmen when the 501st left in June, which turned to splashes of laughter and smiles to greet them on their return. Sims joined in the gaiety of the moment, smiling and waving at the youngsters who waved as they marched past.

The return to England was an arrival at the same base they used before the invasion drop. Some men found themselves in the identical sleeping quarters. It was there that the effects of Normandy invaded their minds. Familiar faces of their friends killed in the fighting were missing, their bunks now conspicuously vacant. Remembered laughter and braggart attitudes of those friends about what they were going to do to the Germans echoed in the air. A somber emptiness set in. They had shared family histories, life dreams for the future, even hearty lies and half-truths with those same men. Those thoughts had been arrested for a time while the battle continued, but the reality of their death was now fully visible. Sadness mingled with the joy for the returning victorious soldiers.

The 101st Airborne Division lost 868 paratroopers killed at Normandy and another 2,303 wounded or injured. Missing or captured amounted to another 665 men. Total killed, wounded, injured or missing/captured came to 3,836. Total unit strength on June 4, 1944 was just over 13,000. Normandy had cost the Allies almost 25% of airborne invasion forces. Paratroopers never knew until well after the war that Allied Command had predicted a casualty rate nearer 70% for the Normandy paratrooper invasion.

Favorite pubs and hangouts were to be re-visited, accompanied by a friendly pint of bitters bestowed on them by appreciative Englishmen. Songs broke out in the pubs. Paratroopers began to settle into a routine of garrison life. Replacement weapons, clothing, and supplies were requisitioned. Replacement paratroopers for those killed and wounded began to trickle in, some fresh from the states. Desperately needed, those green replacements were welcomed, but they would not feel part of the unit. Not until they proved themselves in battle.

Normandy veterans talked politely to the rookie replacements at first, not really caring to even learn the new men's names. Instead, replacements were fed stories of the fight at Normandy. Replacements' eyes riveted to hardened faces of the swaggering paratroopers who had survived. Those veterans sat in the same room with the lowly rookies retelling of battles in the dark and ambushes by German tanks. Trips to the local pub found replacements standing off to one side, wishing they were already veterans with their own story to tell. Instead, they clustered in small groups with other new arrivals and watched like envious eyed little boys.

England was for training, too. Paratroopers had to reacquaint themselves with military protocols again. Saluting in combat had been a no-no. It pointed out an officer to any enemy who may be watching through field glasses. Dress codes had been relaxed in combat. Many had worn the same uniform for the entire time he was in France. Boots were muddy and worn, rifles and gear had to be cleaned and refitted with new parts where needed. Marching in close order drill had gone the way of the salute at the battlefront. Much was to be accomplished in rebuilding a military presence in the paratroopers. England was just the place to complete the job. They had inspections, practiced drill on open fields, polished shoes and boots, washed and pressed uniforms, washed and scrubbed building floors and practiced parachute rigging and jump procedures.

As July shifted into a hot August, the 501st prepared for several missions that did not take place. The Allies were moving across France so quickly that before an operation could gain life the Allies were past the objectives of that mission. One operation after another was cancelled. The entire 101st felt like all they did was prepare for a mission and call it off the next day. Still, they rehearsed and practiced to keep a combat readiness edge.

September arrived. More operations were designed then cancelled. It seemed to the paratroopers that they would not get back to the fight at all if the Germans kept getting defeated so quickly at each battle. But General Dwight Eisenhower and General Montgomery had other plans for the 101st. Operation Market Garden. Behind German lines.

OPERATION MARKET GARDEN

HOLLAND

★ ★ ★ ★ ★ ★

The Holland Invasion

"Glances of true beauty can be seen in the
faces of those who live in true meekness."
- Henry David Thoreau

The Normandy invasion took a heavy toll on the
501st, but replacements had been integrated into the
regiment and rehearsed often enough to become part
of the team. Those replacements would have to prove
themselves in combat before the veteran paratroopers
could allow them to become part of the family. Time
would show their readiness to join the 101st. Holland
would test their mettle.

Why Holland and why now? To understand the
tactical significance of Holland to the Allies, it is
necessary to keep a clear picture of Western European
geography. To reach Holland by boat from the Atlantic
Ocean, one must plot a northeast route through the
English Channel. France would be on the right, England
on the left. After passing France, Belgium is next on the
right, then Holland. The landscape of Holland has no
mountains, thereby leaving the small country relatively
flat from border to border. Roughly five percent the size

of the United States, Holland has a population density higher than the U.S., centered mainly in or around major metropolitan areas.

Germany aggressively and successfully invaded Holland in 1940. Dutch Jews suffered the wrath of Hitler's desire to rid the world of all Jews. He had over one hundred thousand Dutch Jews executed. While that atrocity was taking place, German forces placed rigid controls on the population of Holland. However, the Dutch formed an effective and intelligent underground system they knew would come into play at sometime in the future. German military commanders had no idea the depth of local citizens' commitment to drive the Germans from Holland. Only when American and British forces started collecting intelligence from the Dutch did Allied forces understand the native population's hatred for Germans.

During the early 1940's, Germany used the ports at Antwerp to re-supply and equip German forces in France. For over four years, Germany had free range to the English Channel and shipping lanes via Holland. Allied command saw those same ports as vital portals to re-supply forces in the trek to Germany, which would lessen German presence on the seas as an extra bonus if a successful Dutch campaign could flourish.

With the completed Normandy invasion, Allied troops moved swiftly through France, then into Belgium, pushing the Germany military machine into a hasty retreat towards the homeland. Allied positions advanced so quickly that supplying the front line troops with ammunition, food, and war supplies strained the capabilities of even the best-laid plans. If the Allies could capture and use the port of Antwerp, re-supply problems would ease. The American First Army had been successful in pushing the Germans out of portions of France and Belgium. The British Second Army near the Dutch border was poised along the Escaut Canal, and the American Third Army was nearing Nancy, France. Allied Command did not expect a stout defense by Germany in crossing Holland. The terrain was criss-crossed by canals and rivers, offering German units small defensible positions for delaying actions. The Allies captured Antwerp and placed Hitler in a dilemma. He needed that port facility.

Perhaps the most desirable reason to select Holland was that it represented a direct land access route to German soil with the fewest natural barriers, such as mountains and steep valleys, for an invasion route. The Russians were fully engaged with Hitler's forces on the eastern front. Germans would have few combat units to the west and north to effectively mount counterattacks from that direction, and Allied units were in control of Holland's eastern borders.

A swift run up the main north-south highway of Holland could conceivably put Allied forces inside Germany in a matter of months, maybe weeks. Holland was to become less a war over land possession and more of one over roadways. Allied airborne forces would act as the security units to cover the roadways as other friendly forces traveled up the road. The Allies had air superiority, so not much was thought about German air defense capability.

The overall strategy was this: American and British forces under Montgomery were to dash across Holland, cutting off German retreat lines, support capability, and communication lines. Such an action would also demoralize German ground troops. It was seen as a bold maneuver, but one that could end the war with Hitler far quicker by isolating his forces on the western front and defeating them one at a time. If the Allies could accomplish this task, the push into mainland Germany could come within months, perhaps earlier, saving countless lives while shortening the war. The risk was worth the gamble. An overland attack to control the north-south highways through Holland meant Allied forces could isolate and destroy a vital part of Hitler's military might. Failure could delay the war for an undetermined amount of time. Very little margin of error was available. If any phase of Operation Market Garden failed, the entire push into Germany could stagger and fall, as well as costing many Allied lives.

Allied high command called for the paratroopers to jump ahead of British ground forces. Each airborne was assigned specific points of geography to secure, specifically bridges across main waterways and canals. These bridges could support heavy armor traffic and would be crucial in any speedy advance by Allied ground forces. The 1st British Airborne Division, 82nd Airborne Division, 101st Airborne Division, and the 1st Polish Paratroop Brigade would participate in the jump.

British ground units would charge forward to meet the paratroopers and proceed northeast to rout the German army back towards Germany. The paratroopers would provide flank security up the highway for the advance. Surprise played a part in the plan, but the main thrust was to keep the Germans on defense, not allowing them to regroup and counterattack. Ambitious? Yes. Would it work? Maybe. If British forces did not arrive within three days to meet the paratroopers, there was little hope that the paratroopers could survive. Airborne units did not jump with combat supplies to last more than a few days.

Operation Market Garden was to be the largest parachute invasion in history. British and American forces were tossing all their airborne units into the assault. It would be a day jump with more than 5,000 planes and a combined force of 30,000 airborne paratroopers. Normandy had taught Allied commanders what could go wrong in a night jump. Market Garden would start on September 17, 1944.

The airborne assault was responsible for the southern sector of the north-south highway that ran between Eindhoven and Arnhem, a distance of 60 miles. The southern most section of the highway, from Eindhoven to Grave, would fall under the assignment of the 101st Airborne Division. The midsection, from Grave to Nijmegen, fell to the 82nd Airborne Division, and the northern sector, Arnhem, was the responsibility of British and Polish forces. Each unit of the air assault was to capture and hold the bridges crossing the rivers and canals in their sector until British land forces arrived. The battle plan sounded simple and straightforward, but there would be German strongholds and heavy resistance at several points, especially where German artillery batteries were concentrated. Allied command knew this and counted on the paratroopers to hold out and complete their assignments, even under heavy German artillery and mortar attacks.

In England, Hugo Sims and the balance of the 501st PIR readied themselves for the mission. By September 14, all officers had been alerted to the plan, at least the plan in its roughest draft. Another day would pass before details and drop zones were passed down through the ranks. Sims had been promoted and was now S-2 for the 501st Regiment. Major Richard Allen had also been promoted to regimental staff as S-3. Sims still reported to Allen, and they would be together again on this newest campaign. That suited Sims fine. Having served together during the Normandy campaign, Sims and Allen had established not only a good working relationship, but each had gained a deep friendship with the other during the process.

Sims now had the responsibility of gathering intelligence for the 501st. He would be expected to know, or find out, German information necessary to carry out their orders, no small task since they were headed into unknown territory. He would need to learn what German units they faced, German strength levels, artillery support levels, and stacks upon stacks of information for regimental command as they moved. Sims gathered all the maps he could. He studied terrain features, river crossings, house and farm locations on the map. He reviewed the latest available intelligence information gathered by ground, air, and Dutch underground forces available.

As Sims put it, "Our airplanes did a good job of taking aerial photographs of Holland. We used those photographs many times in locating specific places we thought critical to the objective." Aerial photography had previously been sketchy, both in numbers and quality. Sims learned a great deal more before Operation Market Garden than he had known before Normandy.

The night before their departure, September 16, saw a different tone to the landscape around Newbury in rural Dorset, England. For the past four years, German bombs had fallen in the quiet farms and villages of southern England. The English had grown accustomed to the nightly fear of planes overhead. As a consequence, lights were switched off and curtains were drawn tightly over windows when candles or lanterns had to be lit. For the past four years, England spent nights under total darkness. No street lights, no lamps in store windows, and no lights to be seen after dark. On the night of September 16, Hugo Sims noticed a difference. The lights were on in England.

The morning of Sunday, September 17, was overcast early. Fog and clouds evaporated by midmorning. As paratroopers loaded into the C-47 aircraft, there was the usual complaining and joking around, the banter of men in tense situations. Stomachs tightened, but not like that windy night in June when Normandy was their target. Today they were veterans. Today's stomach tightening was from a sense of urgency to get on with the mission. Normandy had taught them new tricks of the trade. They knew what gear to store, and they knew the best way to store it away for combat jumps. Gear that was strapped on was double checked to ensure it would still be with them when they hit the ground. No night problems on this jump, so the paratroopers would not need the crickets to locate their unit members upon landing on Dutch soil.

In single file, they started the long loading process. As a paratrooper struggled to climb the five steps into the C-47, hands reached out to push him upwards through the doorway. Other hands reached down from the aircraft doorway to help pull the struggling paratrooper inside. The same procedure had taken place before the Normandy campaign.

Major Allen recalled, "In Normandy we had the men file through a large tent where we had placed on tables all the supplies and extra ammo each man was to take. We told them, for example, to take four hand grenades. In normal military fashion, enlisted men went through the line and took six or eight grenades and stuffed them into whatever pockets had room." Smiling at the memory, Allen continued, "Before we took off, the men would throw away items they thought they wouldn't need. They didn't want to carry the extra weight. Some men tossed their gas masks, saying the Germans wouldn't use gas. The pack that stored the gas masks provided a perfect container for extra grenades or bandoliers of ammo. It got out of hand."

Allen learned from that experience. "Before we took off for Normandy, the pilot of our plane, a young second lieutenant, watched as the over packed and heavy paratroopers struggled to board the aircraft. Some were so heavy they had to be pushed up the ladder by other men on the ground. The pilot was afraid the plane wouldn't take off under such a heavy load. I was afraid they weighed too much for the parachute. Each man could weigh no more than a total of 300 pounds, the maximum load of the chute. Any more and a panel of the T-4 parachute could rip out." Allen smiled again, "Some men looked like they weighed way more than the limit, so we monitored them closer loading gear in Holland."

Methodically and with practiced precision, the planes were loaded and ready to take to the air. Engines revved and coughed as they warmed to operating temperature. Though it took more than an hour, all planes were airborne and in formation, heading towards the English Channel for the crossing into Holland.

The flight was more like their training flights. Men could see out windows into the bright daylight. They saw the English countryside, slowly slipping by beneath them, rolling hills and neat farm fields with hedged borders. Next, they passed over London and watched the British shoreline approach and then disappear to reveal open stretches of water of the English Channel below. The white cliffs of Dover could be seen on their left as the planes cleared the coast. This time the water was blue instead of ink black like that night on June 6. The armada of planes stretched for miles in the sky. Fighter planes flew escort to protect them should the Germans send out interceptors. Clouds broke up more, revealing blue sky and bright sunshine.

Conversation that had been rowdy and boisterous only a short time earlier turned to silence as they neared the German occupied territory on the opposite side of the Channel. Paratroopers remembered the flak. They recalled the machine gun tracer rounds. They remembered the explosions. Most of all they remembered the chaos. Normandy returned to their minds in a shocking instant with the arrival of the first few rounds of flak. Only this time, they could see the little black puffs of smoke of antiaircraft rounds when they exploded nearby in the clear daylight.

Fighter planes dived and circled, ever searching for German aircraft. Paratrooper eyes looked nervously around the tight confines of the C-47. Hands moved unconsciously to check gear straps or parachute rigging. One plane exploded in midair, spewing parts of aircraft and dead bodies into the clear sky. Another plane was hit by flak that rendered it into heaps of metal twisting and turning before crashing to the ground. Some paratroopers exited the wounded aircraft in time to save themselves from the ground explosion, others did not survive.

The pilots held their course, steely eyed and steady, in the flak. They flew straight and level, holding formation with firm hands and a determined attitude. Machine gun rounds again arched from the ground, tracers drawing lines spiraling towards the planes. This would be no Normandy fiasco. This time they proved to be the veterans they were. Normandy had taught them lessons, too. Instead of twisting and weaving to avoid the ground fire pouring up at them, pilots held true to their mission to put the paratroopers right over their proper drop zones. Red lights flashed the get ready signal beside the open door. Paratroopers stood, hooked up, checked their gear, and sounded off, then pulsed toward the open door, ready to jump.

Sims was in his usual slot in the stick, last man out the plane. He was jumping this time with a lighter equipment load. Since it was a daylight jump, most didn't need the special night jump gear. He carried a Tommy gun this time instead of the carbine. It was stored in a canvas bag and strapped underneath his harness straps, across his chest. Most had left their gas masks in England. The plane rocked back and forth from unseen air currents, but the pilot held the controls and steadied it quickly. Sims shifted his weight in the bumping motion, ready to move to the door. He glanced up at the signal lights at the door and saw the red light switch off and the green light appear. An instant later, the jumpmaster's voice roared, "Go!"

One by one, the men tossed themselves into the sky. Sims approached the door and without really noticing the view, plunged into the open space outside. Seconds passed, then the familiar jolt of the main parachute opening snapped him upright. Quickly looking up, he saw his chute fully deployed. Looking down, Sims remembered, "I saw thousands of paratroopers swinging and swaying towards the ground. I looked to my front and saw thousands more. The sky was full of paratroopers. I could see more jumping from other C-47s further north. It looked like a perfect practice jump." Below him the fields and farms approached. There were no machine guns blasting away at him like in France. He turned his back to the wind and relaxed his knees. Upon impact, he rolled over and stood up. Perfect landing. Quickly, he unbuckled the parachute harness straps and was on his way to form up with regimental staff to begin the mission. A lone machine gun, distant by the muffled sound, crackled in the afternoon air.

Major Allen jumped first from the same plane as Sims. Allen had made a slight change in his weapon of choice for the Holland jump. "I decided to jump with a

Tommy gun," he recalled. "I tied it off, barrel facing up, on a rope underneath my reserve chute across my chest. It would be ready for me to use when I hit the ground. I had it loaded and ready to go. When the chute opened, the jolt knocked the Tommy gun loose. The only thing holding it was that rope tied around the barrel. It was dangling below my feet. I looked down just before I landed and saw that thing pointed up at me. Then I saw it was going to hit a post and there was nothing I could do but hope it didn't go off when it hit." Allen smiled at the memory, "I was lucky. It hit the post but didn't fire."

Paratroopers on the ground were quickly reassembling with their units, as they had done so many times in practice. The machine gun rattled again in the distance. Other than that, it appeared they had, indeed, caught the Germans by surprise. The 501st hit the ground, formed up into tactical units, and moved toward their objectives in less than thirty minutes. Their drop zone was about three miles northwest of their objective, Vechel. The afternoon sun bore down and the temperature rose. Men sweated heavily, as the air grew stiff and hot. Still, less than four hours after touching down, the 501st had captured Vechel with only light and sporadic German resistance.

Colonel Jumpy Johnson had set up his regimental headquarters in Vechel (rhymes with heckle). He had chosen the home of a Dutch doctor in the village of clean and scrubbed houses. Cheering and happy Dutch citizens ran up and down streets in celebration, offering food and drinks to the paratroopers. The Germans appeared to be nowhere near, or at the least, they were hiding. Sims set up office in the regimental command post, along with

Major Allen, to begin work. The Dutch underground appeared wearing orange armbands to signify their unity with the paratroopers and offered much information to the Americans with great enthusiasm. There were so many in the Dutch underground who came to help that a hired member of their contingent was needed to stand at the door to control ingress and egress.

Sims looked out over the land. "I liked it much better than England or France. Both those countries looked old and tired. Not Holland. Here the country looked more like it did back home. Homes were in excellent shape with fresh paint. Yards were neat and landscaped, even in the middle of German occupation. Bight colors were everywhere."

There was the feeling of happiness and freshness to the people, unlike the dour reception they had received from the French. Sims immediately decided he liked the Dutch. "They were much friendlier and more likeable than the French." The French had been standoffish and uncaring toward the paratroopers. Not until the Germans had been chased clear across France did the French appear friendly, and then only in a reserved fashion. Here in Holland, Dutch citizens appeared to go out of their way to help. The little things counted for so much.

The Dutch offered food when Sims knew they had little to spare. They offered their houses for troops, and did what they could to help. Children and local Dutch citizens ran into the streets to welcome the paratroopers, waving flags and passing out hugs and kisses to the new arrivals. Crowds gathered at street intersections and gave roaring cheers as Allied forces passed.

Holland was no America to Sims, but it was far better than the other countries he had seen so far. The Dutch spirit, laughter and neighborliness, was a lot like being back in South Carolina. Of course, back in his hometown, he did not carry a Tommy gun and wear combat gear. In addition, there were no Germans running around trying to shoot him. However, Holland looked like a country he could adopt as a second home if he were forced to do so.

Holland under siege was still a war zone. All too quickly the Germans would launch counterattacks once the surprise of the assault passed. Until that happened, Sims and the 501st would stand ready and protect the roadways and bridges in their sector. Stiff battles were to come, but now was a time to breathe a little easier. Men ate when they were hungry and cleaned weapons for the fight they knew was coming. Holland was under a euphoric spell for the moment.

The quiet didn't last long. On the morning of September 18, the Germans counterattacked Vechel with tanks and artillery, followed closely by infantry bent on recapturing the small village. Artillery rounds splattered into the town, destroying homes and buildings. Time and time again the paratroopers repulsed the attacks. Street battles raged, sometimes one building to another. German tanks appeared, rumbling and squeaking as they approached. Paratroopers of the 501st stood their ground, blasting away at the tanks with bazookas and anti-tank weapons. Bullets swish-zipped in the air, bouncing off solid surfaces with strange 'zings' and whistling sounds.

Vechel would remain under the control of the 501st, but not without a price. Sims spoke, "Several paratroopers were killed during the day and many injured. At dark the battle continued. Muzzle flashes in the night spread bullets into both German and American positions. Sleep was not in the plan. Skirmishes broke out throughout the town. Tracers from machine guns hit buildings and stone fences. Just as the fight seemed to weaken, it would start again in another location. That went on all night before we were in full command of the town. You could hear German tanks squeaking and clanking in the dark as they tried to get into position."

Vechel became a prognostication of what would follow in Holland. Towns and villages that had been taken became sites of fierce fighting when the Germans counterattacked. Crossroads were usually elevated from the surrounding lowland, making them more susceptible to long rage attack by artillery and tank fire. Mortars lobbed in punctuated the closeness of the fighting on many fronts, followed by bayonet and hand-to-hand combat in many small battles. Both sides knew the enemy was near, but reinforcements for both sides were often too far away to be of immediate help.

Montgomery's British forces did not arrive on schedule, adding to the frustration of the airborne units in Holland. The joyous faces of the Dutch turned again to worried looks after each battle. It was difficult to determine who was ahead in the fight. Montgomery had sent his British ground forces northward, as planned, but delays in arriving at the designated sites placed an extra burden on the isolated paratroopers. All they could do was keep up the fight until someone arrived, British or otherwise, to push the initiative.

Montgomery's plan may have been sound in principle, but it certainly lacked in execution. The British appeared to take a more relaxed attitude in the fighting, opting to take extra time to stop and cook meals alongside the roadways and not risking full assault charges when confronted by the Germans. American paratroopers grew impatient with the slow action of some British units in combat.

Lt. Hugo Sims was not impressed with all the waiting. He saw daily that the Germans could replenish supplies and reinforce combat units if given time. "We could have moved faster if we had more support. We had the Germans on the move, but we had to stop many times because we were too far forward of our support elements. That, and the fact that we were under British command and had to do whatever Montgomery told us to do."

Nijmegen was critical. The bridge there had to be kept open. The 82nd Airborne was having a rough time. British ground forces were to be at Nijmegen by the second day, Monday the 18th. Those forces did not arrive until twenty-four hours later. It was Wednesday, the 20th before the 82nd could clear and capture the bridge at Nijmegen. Allied ground troops crossed the bridge that afternoon.

Down south, the 101st had hard fighting at Best and gave up under a heavy German defense. The southern corridor to British forces was open at Eindhoven and British 30 Corps tanks arrived to help provide security for engineers to build a Bailey Bridge over the Son River because the Germans had blown the original bridge earlier. By Monday the 18th access over the Son was ready for Allied use.

On the northern front all was not well. German forces were far better than information showed in intelligence reports. Preliminary reports showed little or no experienced German troops in the area and few tanks. In fact, there were elements of the Second SS Panzer Corps and two additional Panzer Divisions near Arnhem. Those same early reports stated only a scant 2,000 German personnel, filled mostly with recruits, were left to defend Arnhem. In fact, there were over 6,000 experienced and hardened German troops in the Arnhem area. In addition, the drop zone for the Polish airborne was nearly 15 miles from the bridge and those paratroopers were dropped north of the river in Arnhem. British and Polish paratroopers never gained an upper hand, most being defeated, killed or captured. The full story of what happened on this northern sector is best described in Cornelius Ryan's book, *A Bridge Too Far.*

Throughout the balance of September Allied forces played bodyguard on the north-south highway 69 in Holland. Flanking elements were sent out to guard against German attacks. Patrols steadily pushed both sides of the corridor to stay alert to German movements. Most of the action was artillery attacks, by both sides, and small skirmish actions in isolated cases. Bridgeheads were firmly in control of the paratroopers and the highway itself remained open to ground force troop movements.

Fall would give way to colder weather in October. With the cooler temperatures came rain. It rained a record amount in the fall of 1944 in Holland. Mud was a constant companion to the paratroopers. No heavy trucks or tanks could maneuver to the side of the main roadways without becoming bogged down in the muck, so most fighting action was done at a distance with artillery rounds exploding and splattering mud high into the air.

October 8, 1944, would change the 501st forever. It was mid-morning, near ten o'clock when Colonel Johnson went to the front to inspect the lines. Always a stickler for details, as his veterans recalled from their days at Toccoa when they first trained to become one of Johnson's paratroopers, Johnson wanted the latest information about his men and their situation. The veteran members of the 501st who had jumped into the night sky over Normandy expected Johnson to be near the front. He had always been right in the middle of the action. He led that way, in a style often compared to Patton. To say he loved war may have been an exaggeration, but he dearly loved confrontation on the battlefield.

Johnson arrived to meet Major William Pelham, executive officer of Johnson's 2nd Battalion, and Captain Richard Snodgrass. Artillery fire was sporadic that overcast October morning. A few shells came and went as clouds broke and regrouped. Johnson had great pride in his 501st. They had stood beside him at Hell's Corner at the LaBarquette lock and fought off the massive German artillery attack. They had waited in ambush for the 500 elite German paratroopers on June 7, capturing or killing them all. They had fought like demons at Carentan to hold that vital crossroad city for the Allies. Now, they stood their ground fighting as infantrymen because no help came. Johnson had every right to be proud, and he wanted his men to see him face to face so he could personally tell them how well they did their sometimes-thankless job.

Colonel Johnson and his 501st had been on the ground in Holland for nearly a month without relief. Being under mortar and artillery fire most of that time strained even the stoutest resolve. Attacks by fire came at random, unpredictable and without warning. Sometimes there was only a single round. Other times there were barrages that lasted for hours. Stress became a daily factor, unceasing and uncaring to those who witnessed the dead and wounded from exploding rounds that landed haphazardly around and amongst the paratroopers. Johnson knew their plight. He had been right there among his men during those attacks.

That October morning found Colonel Johnson, Major Pelham and Captain Snodgrass discussing the tactical situation outside 2nd Battalion headquarters under mild but chilly temperatures. Seemingly out of nowhere, an artillery round landed to one side of the three officers. The three officers hesitated in their discussion until the rumble echoed silence. Tendrils of smoke lingered from the explosion. No one had been injured from the artillery round. Johnson and his officers continued their talk. Johnson had been injured during the sand dune fight at Eerde, an ear wound, and his hearing had not fully recovered.

None of the three men were under protective cover and a German artillery observer across the Neder Rijn watched as they stood in the open. Adjusting the artillery fire, he sent another round towards the American forces. Whether or not Johnson's hearing difficulties played a part is not known, but both Pelham and Snodgrass dove to the ground a split second before Johnson, having perhaps heard the artillery round's high-pitched swish-shriek sound. As Johnson was in the process of tossing himself down, the shell burst hit him. Shrapnel and shell fragments ripped into his neck and back. Johnson was quickly carried into the command post.

The battalion surgeon was at Johnson's side in minutes, making the colonel lie still as an examination took place. Starting with the neck wound, the surgeon, Captain Axelrod, began his work. Colonel Johnson, still conscious and talking, said, "My back." As soon as Axelrod checked Johnson's back wound, he scurried upstairs to call for an ambulance to transport the wounded colonel to the hospital in Nijmegen.

Before the ambulance sped off, Johnson had it stop for a minute at his regimental command post, where he had a quick talk with Major Allen and Colonel Ewell. Lieutenant Hugo Sims stood near as they talked. Gravely wounded men in combat often have a premonition if they believe they are not going to live. When that happens, they feel an urge to speak in terms that make a listener feel that sense of approaching death. Johnson spoke a few words about his wife and children, then spoke his last words to anyone connected with the 501st, telling Ewell and Allen, "Take care of my boys." Colonel Howard Johnson died on the way to the hospital on October 8, 1944, on Hell's Highway in Holland.

Word spread fast. Up and down the ranks men were shocked. Their leader, most respected and revered, had been killed. The thought that the Germans could kill Johnson had never entered their thoughts. Somehow, Colonel Johnson seemed to be above that. His tough leadership had taken them from raw citizens to hardened veterans, all the while showing them how leaders inspire men to go beyond their expectations and do what seems impossible. Johnson appeared invincible. Sure, paratroopers could be killed, even the man sharing a foxhole, but not "Jumpy" Johnson. Nearly unbelievable. It just didn't seem possible. But it was.

Leadership of the 501st would fall to Colonel Julian J. Ewell, perhaps one of the most adept tacticians in the 101st. Ewell was already admired by the paratroopers of the 501st, almost universally. There would not be another Johnson, but Ewell was a strong and capable individual with talent and experience. He would lead the 501st with his own individual style without loss of efficiency or resoluteness. Colonel Ewell would surround himself with equally talented officers and staff to build on what Johnson had started.

Paratrooper sadness about Johnson's death would not leave the men, and he would remain in their thoughts the remainder of their lives. Johnson left a legacy they would cherish always. His get-up-and-charge attitude would see them through another impossible task in the coming months, though they did not know it at the time. Colonel Ewell did not want the men to forget. He wanted them to remain steadfast and strong just as Johnson had taught. Ewell, too, felt the loss of a good friend in Johnson's passing. Those first few weeks of October were not easy ones, emotionally or physically for the 501st.

The 501st moved northeast, along with the entire 101st, towards Arnhem, the northeastern perimeter of Allied-held roadways. The original area of responsibility for the

101st did not go up as far as Nijmegen but it was obvious that the northern segment of Operation Market Garden was in trouble. Bridges at Nijmegen and Arnhem had met stiff German resistance. They were both closer to the German war machine and Hitler's reinforcements and heavy weapon units came down in mass. The British and Polish airborne drops had gone as planned, but they stalled out under heavy German counterattacks. The 101st was moved up in a position to face off with the Germans to help keep the highway open.

Home for the 501st would be in the sector of low, flatland south of the Lower Rhine River and north of the Waal River. The entire area was called the island even though it was not entirely surrounded by water in the normal sense. Between the two rivers the land was lower than the dikes on each river. Threats or rumors that the Germans intended to blow holes in the dikes floated through paratrooper ranks repeatedly. Those threats never came to pass but it did keep American leaders concerned and preparations for a quick exit were designed and ready to implement if necessary.

Sims was between the villages of Heteren and Driel, roughly ten miles west of Arnhem. At his position they were on the south bank of the Lower Rhine. Sims recalled, "We were right beside the dike by the river. If anyone stood on the dike, the Germans could see them from across the river and draw mortar or artillery fire, so we stayed low most of the time during daylight."

The 501st, 502nd and the 506th relieved British forces along this northern perimeter of Allied held territory. The 501st occupied the land along the Lower Rhine, the 502nd anchored the eastern line from Driel to the river just north of Nijmegen, and the 506th occupied the western line from the Waal River through Opheusden and linked up with the western end of the 501st line. British and Polish paratroopers had taken high casualties in their attempt to take Arnhem. Their numbers had been decimated and Allied commanders rushed American paratroopers of the 101st to help to ward off any German offensive until infantry units could arrive.

Opheusden became the focal point for some of the most bitter fighting in Holland. A railroad bed, elevated five feet above ground level, ran north out of Nijmegen, then swung west to cross the Lower Rhine after passing Opheusden. The town was just north of the railroad and about three thousand yards south of the Lower Rhine. During the first week of October, German troops gathered in force to attack from west to east, their ultimate goal to recapture Nijmegen.

On October 5 the German offensive began. The 506th bore the brunt of the fight at and around Opheusden. For nearly a week the battle seesawed back and forth. Each German attack encountered a resolute element of the 506th determined to hold their ground. Early in the battle losses by the 506th were light but as the battle progressed those casualties became larger in number and frequency. The fight continued until the 9th when the 327th arrived to give the battered but successful 506th a deserved rest. The 327th found the fighting as bitter as any they encountered in all of Holland.

The surrounding area was embattled to a stand off between American and German forces by October 15th.

It became a no-man's land patrolled by both sides, owned by neither. Heavy rains came on the 13th and 14th, adding a slippery and slick mud to footing and filling foxholes with knee-deep water. Men sat wet as fish. The weather and the enemy restricted movement. By the end of the fight, Opheusden had become the largest single battle of the island campaign in Holland.

Sims was not involved with the Opheusden battle but his 501st line of defense was linked up with the right flank of the 506th. Sims sent out constant patrols to ensure their flanks were not vulnerable. The Lower Rhine provided a safety to their front. The logical weak point was on the left if the Germans chose to attack the flank. Many night patrols were sent out to be specifically alert for any sign of a German build-up near their sector. "We heard the battle," Sims remembered, "but our orders were to secure our positions along the river. That's what we did."

October drew to a close. Sims and the 501st maintained their position on the Lower Rhine. The fierce fighting lingered in isolated battles and firefights but most German activity was artillery and mortar actions against the 101st across their front.

THE INCREDIBLE PATROL

"The best way to escape from a problem is to solve it"
- Alan Saporta

Patrol action continued as the 501st dug in on the eastern bank of the Lower Rhine River, less than 10 miles northeast of Arnhem. German occupied territory was across the river and Allied troops knew little of German manpower numbers or troop and artillery movements. German and American soldiers could see each other across the Rhine, just out of rifle range. A guarded tenseness hung in the air. Each side knew the other was fully capable of artillery and mortar attacks at any moment and each was unsure what might come next. The threat of an all-out attack was constant.

American commanders were running patrols up and down the Lower Rhine with little success. Incoming mortars and heavy artillery continued to be the most stout German attack mode. Casualties grew at a slow but steady pace. Small skirmishes between German and paratrooper units continued. Sims remembered the shelling vividly, "We were dug in along the side of the river. It was still really wet from all the rain. When an artillery round landed you could see big chunks of dirt and mud flying everywhere. Moving vehicles and heavy tracked trailers was darn near mpossible in all that mud. We just kept our heads down and waited."

Colonel Ewell, now the commanding officer of the 501st following Johnson's death, had little or no accurate German intelligence information. Patrols gathered nothing new and what information did come in was without substance. He could offer no news to Division about their enemy across the river. His men were holding the ground they occupied and tossing artillery and mortars back at the Germans but did not know how effective their efforts were.

Hugo Sims, as S-2, headed the intelligence-gathering unit for the 501st. He sent out patrols on a daily basis and was as disappointed as was Colonel Ewell at the lack of positive results. Sims felt he had good men in the S-2 section. He wasn't skeptical about their ability but he was angered that patrols returned with little information worthy of the effort. By late October the weather changed to the colder fall wind and a steady dose of rain. That didn't help the spirits of men who were assigned to go on patrol.

General Gerald Higgins, the Executive Officer of the 101st Airborne Division, visited the 501st to see the front line for himself. In Colonel Ewell's absence, Sims met with General Huggins and remembered the incident well. "General Higgins met with me about the middle of the morning. He told me it was imperative that we find out what German units were opposing us so that headquarters could determine whether the Germans were moving troops out toward another area or if they were moving more units into our area. He thought the best way to find out was to capture a German prisoner so we could interrogate him."

Higgins asked, "Sims, can you get me a prisoner?"

Sims replied a simple, "Yes, Sir."

Over the next ten days Sims sent out patrol after patrol with the single instruction, "Bring back a prisoner." None were successful.

Sims grew tired of excuses and negative results. "I knew the Germans were just across the river in plain sight during the day. How could anyone not capture a single prisoner at night? I finally decided that the patrols were not doing their job. I later discovered that some patrols crossed the river and slept in hiding until time to come back across the river. They never went far enough to see a German, much less capture one."

Out of frustration Sims decided to go out and get the prisoners himself. In a written authorization request to conduct the patrol, Sims sent Colonel Ewell a message, finalizing with, "I feel that this patrol is necessary as a stimulus for the battalions."

Colonel Julian Ewell replied in large letters across the request, "OK, J.J.E." there were no other instructions or comments.

S-2

MEMO: For your information.

TO : Commanding Officer

Reconnaissance Patrol To Leave Night of 30-31 October:

1. Purpose:
        a. To determine the practicability of patrols
being guided by artillery fire.
        b. To determine the practicability of using
flares in close coordination with patrols.
        c. To determine if the enemy has an MLR.
        d. To observe a main axis of communication to
determine direction and density of traffic.
        e. To identify unit or units opposing us.

2. Composition:
        a. Patrol leader: Lt. H. S. Sims
        b. Asst. Patrol leader: Cpl. Canfield
        c. Three riflemen: From Regt. S-2 Section.
        d. German speaker: From PW team.

3. Mission: to establish an observation post during
the hours of darkness in the enemy rear area; to observe
enemy activity during the following day.

4. I feel that this patrol is necessary as a stimulus for the Battalions.

H. S. SIMS,
1st Lt., 501 Prcht Inf
Intelligence Officer

OK JJE

Sims asks permission to lead the Incredible Patrol

Photocopy of the original request to go on what
would be published as "The Incredible Patrol" in Life
magazine in their January 1945, edition. Sims outlined
the procedures he would follow and why the patrol
was necessary. Note the handwritten approval of
"OK, J.J.E." approval by Colonel Julian Ewell, Sims'
commanding officer. (Photocopy courtesy Mark Bando)

Sims was elated. "I was a little shocked. Usually there were more instructions and a request to write out everything and get it approved at several levels. This time there was just the go-ahead."

First Lieutenant Hugo Sims had never before in his military life been given such freedom. Most military missions were filled with orders about what to do, where to go, and how to do everything while on the mission. Specific goals and objectives were usually stated, with secondary backup plans, in detail, about procedures and processes if the initial goals could not be met. Not this time. Sims had the liberty, the unheard of freedom, of developing a plan to execute the entire patrol without intervention from any other authority. He could choose the members of the patrol at his discretion. This was almost too good to be true. Now, if he was going to pull it off and not have egg on his face afterwards, he would need to come up with a plan that was effective, discreet, and most of all, a plan to survive the patrol.

The Incredible Patrol, as it became known worldwide, was entirely the brainchild of Lt. Hugo Sims. An account of that patrol was penned by Corporal Russ Engel and published in *Life Magazine* in January of 1945. While factual in most regards, there were some critical omissions and a few discrepancies printed. Until now, no account of that patrol, led by Sims himself, has ever been written after interviewing Sims. The original account was written within days of the actual patrol. Mr. Engel visited the 501st to interview patrol members for the article after hearing about it through the military grapevine, scuttlebutt as it was called. He wanted to check it out for himself. As a news writer prior to the war, he was a competent author. As a member of the 101st Airborne Division, he had little trouble in getting permission for the task of writing about the patrol.

Engel gathered five members of the patrol in a small room in regimental headquarters and let them tell him the story. Each man contributed to the telling, each in his own words, as Engel feverishly wrote each word down for the record. There was one flaw in his process. The patrol consisted of six men, not five. The only man left out of the interview process, and, therefore, his input omitted, was none other than the man responsible for coming up with the idea, planning the entire patrol, then leading it out and back, Lt. Hugo Sims. Sims was back at the Division hospital having dental work performed. With such a fine reputation as a writer, it is puzzling why Engel did not contact Sims, even if it meant an additional trip to meet and speak with the man. In light of Sims' absence, it follows that errors and omissions may have crept into the retelling of the patrol. Indeed, that very consequence happened.

Upon receiving Ewell's approval, Sims began planning the entire operation. He gathered maps of the area he would patrol. His plan was to cross the Lower Rhine in rubber boats after dark, slip behind enemy lines and hide in a house he had located on the map beside the Utrecht-Arnhem highway. He could watch and record German troop and supply movements on the highway during daylight hours, then capture a German prisoner or two and return the following night. With the overall plan finished, Sims worked on the details.

High on the priority list was stealth. If the patrol was to succeed, they could not afford to be detected. His thoughts went immediately to a small but significant factor: headgear. The American combat helmet was easily seen, even in the darkness, because it had rigid, stiff lines, clearly different from any surrounding terrain features. Sims tossed them aside for soft caps. As Sims pointed out, "Soft covers were hard to see at night and they made no noise if a stick or twig brushed against them."

Next, Sims reviewed weapons. He had decided that he would take five men, plus himself, on the patrol. If they were detected or seen, a small unit such as the patrol would find it necessary to break contact and get out fast if they were to survive. A prolonged firefight could spell disaster. That meant they would need as much firepower as possible for such a small unit. Sims chose the Tommy gun as his weapon of choice. He would give patrol members a choice of weapons. "I had decided on the Tommy gun as my choice." Standard machine guns with the heavy tripod and extra ammo boxes were out of the question for a stealth-driven patrol. He next added four hand grenades and knives for each man and sprinkled in a few illumination and smoke grenades in case they were needed.

Sims would need to navigate the path to and from the selected house beside the highway in the dark of night. There was no margin for error. If Sims made a mistake in navigation, they could all end up dead. He sat down and studied the maps again, plotted the correct azimuth from the river crossing point to the house and wrote down the coordinates, then paid a visit to the officer in charge of the regimental artillery unit. Sims instructed the officer to fire two white phosphorus artillery rounds every fifteen minutes at a specific clump of trees on the map. Plotting the location of the trees from the targeted house, he could use the flash from the exploding artillery round as a reference point, allowing Sims to adjust his direction of travel to correct any error in his pathway direction. This would assure Sims he would arrive at his chosen location.

Sims had to consider his next problem: cover and concealment. He simply could not leave to chance the possibility of being seen during the patrol. American forces sent out patrols on a regular basis at night. Sims knew the Americans had become creatures of habit in policies and procedures for these patrols. It was standard procedure for front line combat units to shoot up flares every twenty minutes or so over enemy positions to provide light enough to see if the enemy was moving about or gathering in force for a potential attack. The only time American forces did not fire up a flare was when the Americans had a patrol out. They didn't want the enemy to see the patrols when an American flare went up.

Sims said, "I figured the Germans were smart enough to notice that pattern, so I instructed the artillery officer to fire up an illumination flare at specified time intervals. I would synchronize my watch before leaving. Two minutes before a flare was to go up, I'd have the men lie down and observe what was happening in the area ahead of them. This would lessen the chance the patrol would walk up unexpectedly on Germans in the dark. I hoped the flares going up would also keep German alertness at a low level, thinking no American patrols were in the area."

Finally, Sims had to consider the most crucial element of the patrol: the participants, "I knew the patrol had, at best, only a fifty-fifty chance that a patrol member would come back alive. We were going six miles behind German lines, in the middle of the night, into an area nobody knew anything about, except what was on the old maps. I needed men I could count on. That was not the time to break in a new man." Sims would make this an all-volunteer patrol. No member could be ordered to participate in a patrol with chances of survival so low. Sims would lean heavily towards his own S-2 men first.

One thing was certain. Smiling in the recollection, Sims spoke quietly but with conviction, "I wanted Corporal William (R.) Canfield as the assistant patrol leader. Canfield was as steady and competent as they came. There wasn't any better man than Canfield." Sims contacted Canfield and explained the mission, advising Canfield that it was strictly a volunteer mission. Canfield, from Selman, Okalahoma, quickly accepted. Sims then told Canfield the idea was that as each new man was selected, he would then participate in selecting the remaining volunteers.

One additional resource was a requirement as far as Sims was concerned. "I needed someone who spoke fluent German. A German speaking member of the patrol could communicate with prospective prisoners, and could attempt to talk the patrol out of a tight situation if confronted by Krauts in the dark." The prisoner interrogation unit had such a man. Master Sergeant Peter R. Frank, from New York City, had asked Sims on other missions to let him go on a patrol. This would be his chance to come along. Canfield and Sims met with Frank and disclosed the plan. Sims smiled again, "Frank didn't waste any time in accepting."

Sims, Canfield, and Frank then chose the next man, Private First Class Fredrick J. Becker, of Atlantic, Iowa. Becker was a quiet paratrooper, but Sims had great respect for his efficiency. All three men met with Becker, who excitedly joined in. The last two members of the patrol were brought in the same way. Private Roland J. Wilbur, of Lansing, Michigan, and Private Robert O. Nicolai, of Midlothian, Illinois. Nicholai was well known as a top-notch paratrooper, especially in a tight spot. Wilbur had the same reputation, but in addition, his marksmanship skills were among the best in the 501st. Wilbur chose his favorite weapon, the M-1. All the others went for the Tommy gun.

Patrol member selection complete, Sims now went into rehearsals with them all. "Each man had to know the plan in case something happened to the leaders during the patrol. Everyone had to know each man's job. Each understood the importance of cover, concealment and stealth. Each man knew he might not return." Above all, each man had respect and faith in the others. After all, lives hung in that trust. Sims recalled the preparation, "We rehearsed over and over. Every detail was practiced, the route shown over and over on the maps, and azimuths plotted again and again for accuracy." Sims knew the men. They were ready.

Sims discussed the patrol with Major Allen beforehand. Allen was not so certain the patrol could add as much value as Sims' expectations. Allen recalled some of the talks, "I told Hugo that hiding in a house beside the highway and watching vehicles might not be of much intelligence value. All he would see was vehicle traffic and I didn't see how that would give us much more than we already knew." Allen smiled in the memory, "He was determined to make it work and I didn't try to talk him out of it."

On a chilly last night in October the patrol left the relatively secure confines of their regimental base camp. Major Allen recalled, "The patrol would cross the river through my lines and return the same way the following night. We would be the unit to see them leave and return."

The sky was dark by 7:30 that night with just a sliver of moon hung in the partially cloudy sky as the patrol loaded their equipment. Sims took a breath as he recalled, "We put everything into two jeeps and drove down to the dike by the river." From there the patrol members slipped down to the banks of the Lower Rhine. Scattered cumulous clouds drifted across the shallow moonlight above. Sims, Canfield and one other patrol member quietly entered one rubber boat.

Just before shoving off, Sims held up his hand, gesturing for everybody to freeze. Sims' eyebrows squinted, "I heard a sound from across the river. Rain began to fall on us as we stooped in the darkness. After a few tense minutes of waiting in the shadows, I didn't hear anything else so I gave the signal to shove the boat away from the bank." The first boat would cross the fifty-yard wide river to the opposite side before the second one launched. Once both boats had delivered the patrol members to the German side, boat handlers returned to the American side of the river. They would not see the patrol members until the patrol returned the next night and flashed a light three times as the signal to come back across to pick them up.

When the boats returned safely across the river, Sims took one last look back. Recalling, "It would be more than twenty-four hours before we stood a chance of seeing any friendly forces again, but there was no time for second-guessing and no turning back."

Sims had heard his fellow officers' taunting remarks before he left his quarters to go on the patrol. They thought he was crazy. Captain Les Cady, a fellow officer and friend of Sims, advised him, "Hugh, you are doing a very foolish thing." Another friend, Major Roberts, the regimental operations officer, echoed the same sentiments, "Poor Huey, age 1," making reference to Sims' son. Sims had heard their words, and he had great faith in those fellow officers' opinions. Sims also had another faith and trust in his own confidence and ability. He was not in agreement with their assessment.

The night was misty dark. Carefully and with all the stealth they could gather, the patrol started toward the German lines. If they were seen, there was no way they could get back to the river and get across without being shot or captured. Each step was a calculated risk. Each patrol member kept low, looking from one side to the other, listening for any sound out of place. Sims kept them on the correct heading until they came to a pond. Sims remembered the pond, "It was too deep and too wide to wade across so we skirted the pond. We waded in ankle-deep water several times."

Sims had carefully chosen a route on the maps that would allow him to observe as much German activity as possible, while affording the men the most cover and concealment in the covert patrol. He had speculated they would need to travel northwest first, then skirt around Wolfeeze and veer back to the northeast after passing the quiet little Dutch hamlet. They should reach the selected house by the highway well before daylight, providing they did not have to face off with German troops in a firefight.

Sims had a wrinkle in his brow as he thought back, "I had a plan if we encountered Germans in the dark. I had instructed Sgt. Frank to claim we were out looking for a sick relative. I hoped that Frank could be convincing enough to avoid raising concern and we could continue the patrol. If it came to a fight, we were prepared to open fire at a moment's notice, then light out toward the American side of the river."

Movement in the darkness was a cautious step-by-step procedure. Each step was followed by a short pause to listen for sounds that did not belong in the night. Night vision was stunted some by the flares going off on schedule during the darkness, but each man strained to see all he could by constantly scanning from one side to another, watching for shapes or movement.

Sims constantly checked his watch. At precisely two minutes prior to the launch time for a flare, he motioned his patrol members down in the wet and marshy grass. They would watch, unmoving, as the flare erupted in the air, watching the surroundings for any sign of Germans. The flare, attached to a small parachute, dangled and swung back and forth with the light breeze as it descended.

Illumination was a faded white/yellow color light that caused shadows of trees and tall bushes to dance with the motion of the glowing flare. As the light from the fluttering flare went out, Sims motioned his men up again and continued toward his objectives. He was certain the balance of the night would not go as smoothly as this first segment of the patrol. As each minute passed, they moved further and further behind German lines. When they reached the house, if they reached it at all, they would be fully six miles behind German lines, a sobering thought. If they needed help, none would be available.

Sims chose to focus on succeeding, not on the what-ifs. Centering his thoughts along the positive line, he was able to plan as he went. If a German prisoner was seen early in the patrol, no attempt would be made to capture him. Sims had already made a decision on that. "I chose not to take any prisoners early. Other Germans would miss the prisoner and our best chance for success was not being seen or heard by anyone. Besides, we would have the added duty of watching the prisoner for a longer period of time, a risky tactic when isolated behind enemy lines. Plus, a prisoner would be constantly looking for a way to escape or sound an alarm." Sims wasn't about to take unnecessary risks, not this early.

Within the first hour after crossing the river the patrol encountered a dim light ahead and sounds of voices of German troops. Sims stopped the men and after a whispered discussion directed them around the sounds. Germans would be anywhere, much the same as it would be to hear Americans moving about behind their lines. Sims quietly led the patrol in a wide path to avoid potential discovery or confrontation. He retraced his path towards the American lines until he felt safe to circle wide around the noises.

In the published version of the Incredible Patrol in *Life Magazine*, one member of the patrol stated that about this time the patrol came upon a sleeping German in the woods. According to the Life story, the paratrooper wanted to take the sleeping German prisoner, but Sims refused the request. When asked about this incident, Sims smiled, "I think that was a slight embellishment on the part of that paratrooper. Sometimes men tend to add a little spice in the retelling of a story like the patrol." Slowly shaking his head from side-to-side, he continued, "It didn't happen." This inconsistency may have been avoided if the original author had interviewed Sims at the time he spoke with other members of the patrol.

The *Life Magazine* article relates the story of the patrol's sighting an ammunition dump while moving through German lines that night. The *Life* story states that one member, Sgt. Peter Frank, crept up to the containers to read the German inscriptions printed on the boxes. Frank supposedly returned to report what was in the containers and Sims was reported as writing down the items to report back to the Allies on the radio later.

Sims recalled the incident, "We spotted a location with assorted sized containers, but we couldn't tell what was in them. I didn't send anyone forward to inspect writing on containers. That would have been too risky. But I did write down the map coordinates and noted it was a suspected German ammunition or supply point."

The *Life* article also reported the sighting and fairly substantial investigation of a truck depot area later that same night. Sims partially agreed, "We saw a number of trucks, but it was no more than a parking place, probably for the night, rather than a full-fledged depot. My opinion was that it might have been only a temporary fueling point for German vehicles in the area, like a mobile service station. I marked it on my map and we circled around it."

There is a point in the *Life Magazine* story where one patrol member, PFC Robert O. Nicholai is relating the incident when the patrol approached a house, which was intended for their occupation as they watched for traffic along the Arnhem-Utrecht highway. Nicholai is quoted as saying, "We all waited a few minutes at the side of the road while Lieutenant Sims brought out a map and checked our location. We were right behind a house that marked the exact spot where we had planned to hit the road. This was only luck."

Luck? Sims had poured over all the aerial maps available and selected that exact house because it afforded the patrol an undetected access to observe highway traffic. Sims had plotted the exact compass heading and azimuths to get to that house, instructed artillery to fire timed rounds to explode on a specified target so he could adjust his patrol directions while in route, checked to make sure he stayed on the planned route, and arrived on schedule at the prescribed location. Luck had nothing to do with it. The patrol arrived because of skilled leadership carried out by the man responsible for the entire mission: Lt. Hugo Sims. PFC Nicholai was hand picked by Sims because of his skills. Nicholai was not given access to all the pre-patrol preparation that went into planning. Execution of that plan was not the responsibility of Nicholai. That, too, was delegated to Sims.

Sims picked up the story again, "I chose to skirt Wolfeeze so we could get to the designated house along the highway on schedule and then crossed a railroad track. There were lots of German troops in that town. We came out on the highway and I checked the map to be sure we were in the right spot. When we reached the house I sent two men to check it out. Discovering that the house was empty presented another problem. If we went inside and occupied the house, Germans may notice activity in the house they believed vacant and decide to investigate. I needed all the daylight hours to observe traffic on the highway. That was part of the objective, so staying in a vacated house was another high risk. I knew we needed to find another location, so we went further down the highway."

"We went another mile, maybe a little more, down the Arnhem-Utrecht highway," Sims recalled' "and found several small houses, one with a tiny Red Cross insignia on the side. It appeared to be the better choice, so I sent Nicholai and Sgt. Frank to investigate. As the two men approached they heard the sound of snoring coming from inside the house. They went steadily towards the rear of the house and discovered a door unlocked. Slowly easing through the door, both paratroopers saw two German soldiers sound asleep on a bed of straw."

Nicholai recalled, "They wore big, shiny boots and I was sure they were officers. Sergeant Frank said they were cavalrymen. Leaving Frank on guard, I went back outside and reported to Lieutenant Sims. He said we would take the men prisoners and stay at this house. I told Frank the plan and he began to shake the Germans. One of them finally began to rub his eyes. He stared at us and Frank kept telling him over and over that he was a prisoner. They just couldn't believe it."

Sims and the remaining members of the patrol then entered the house. Sims retold, "I went upstairs and set up the radio so we could report observations back to our command units. Frank interrogated the captured German soldiers and gave the information to me. I contacted the American forces back across the Lower Rhine and told them, 'This is Sims, Sims. We have two prisoners. We have two prisoners'." Sims then proceeded to relay the information about what they had observed on the route to the house.

Further interrogation of the prisoners by Frank divulged the Germans were expecting another German soldier to pick them up at about 5:30 in the morning. Sims assigned guards for the prisoners and set up watches to observe traffic passing by on the highway outside. They would wait until dark before attempting to move out towards American lines back at the river. The day could be a fruitful one, or it could turn into a nightmare if they were discovered. The clock passed 5:30 and the German prisoners' pick-up man failed to show.

Sims looked at the ceiling and spoke, "At about 7:00 that morning, a young boy wandered into the yard outside and approached the front door. He looked to be about fifteen or sixteen years old and was wearing knee pants. The boy was delighted to be taken prisoner by

'Tommies'. Sergeant Frank took time to explain we were not Tommies, but American paratroopers. The boy told us that the house belonged to family friends and he had come over to get some preserves. The owners had evacuated the house and he knew no one was home."

"More interrogation showed the boy had an older brother in the Dutch underground who had much more intelligence about German activity in the area. He informed us that his brother would also be along in a short while. The boy then gave what information he had about the various German installations nearby, as well as artillery positions and unit numbers. I relayed the new information back to headquarters on the radio." The young boy was telling the truth. A few minutes passed and the brother arrived. Sims spoke again, "The brother had papers showing he was a member of the Dutch underground. He gave us lots of information about German gun locations and pinpointed German units on the map. I radioed the information immediately."

Six more civilians arrived within an hour, a mixture of men and women. They, too, were told they could not leave until the patrol left that night. There was just too much at stake if the patrol's location was discovered. Even though it appeared the civilians posed no threat, Sims decided the risk was too high to allow them to leave. "None of the civilians liked the idea of having to stay," Sims recalled, "but they appeared to be happy to see Americans. They all said they knew the owners were away and came over to get something from the house."

Next, Sims told, "By noon, traffic along the highway heading towards Arnhem increased. Convoys of trucks, filled with supplies and equipment went by at a steady pace. We wrote down what we saw and I would radio it back to headquarters. Then a German soldier entered the courtyard in front of the house to get a drink of water. I don't remember which man it was, but one patrol member pointed the barrel of his Tommy gun out the door and commanded the German to come inside. The German soldier followed the order, laughing as he came inside the house, thinking the whole thing was a joke. He turned out to be a mail orderly who had lost his way while going to another nearby town." Sims smiled at the memory, " He was quickly ushered to a place with the other captive Germans."

Immediately after the arrival of the latest prisoner, someone mentioned food and they all prepared to eat. Patrol members ate K-rations. Sims, as he had done in Normandy, ate a chocolate bar. "The civilians brought out cheese and bread from small bags they had and shared it with everybody," Sims remembered and smiled, "I ate another chocolate bar. I have always liked chocolate. Still do."

Sims thought during the lunch period that some decisions needed to be made. "We had more prisoners than we had planned to capture. The mail carrier would obviously have some valuable information about unit numbers and their locations. The return escape route was clear in my mind, but we still had to come up with transportation to get them back near the river. We would need to move faster than we did the previous night."

As Sims mulled over his options, the German who was supposed to have arrived at 5:30 that morning to meet the original two prisoners showed up in the courtyard with two horses pulling a cart. He proceeded to water the horses. A patrol member called out to him, "Put up your hands, you are a prisoner." He apparently didn't understand, so it was repeated.

The German soldier answered calmly, "I must feed my horses." He finally raised one hand and came towards the house, stating it couldn't be true that he was a prisoner. During his interrogation by Sims, the civilians joined in answering some questions about the local geography since the German didn't know the names of all the little towns nearby.

Two more Germans entered the courtyard. They were immediately captured and brought inside. Sims said, "We now had six German prisoners and another eight civilians in the house, along with our six-man patrol. It was getting a little crowded. I wanted to keep a close watch on the German prisoners so I kept them away from windows and doors." He did not want one of them to raise attention in any manner that could be seen or heard outside, so he placed them fully under the watchful eyes of patrol members.

As darkness approached, Sims had his men gather their equipment. "I left Becker inside the house to guard the prisoners and civilians and then took the rest of the men out to look for a truck for the return trip." The German mail orderly, who had appeared to be the most content with his status as a prisoner, was chosen to go along with Sims. Sergeant Frank would be nearby to make sure anything said was in accordance with Sims' orders.

The highway was in near darkness as Sims and the remaining patrol members stood beside the highway. An entire German company went by on bicycles. German soldiers shouted, "Guten Abend" to the men as they passed, unaware that those men were Americans. It was too dark to distinguish faces and uniforms. One German even stopped and asked Sergeant Frank if this was the correct road to the next town, to which Frank answered in perfect German that he didn't know.

"Time went by without seeing a single vehicle that filled our requirements," Sims wrinkled brow showed, "When we saw several that did, there were too many German forces nearby to attempt capturing the truck. I knew we couldn't wait too long. More vehicles passed, but we didn't see any we could use." Sims glanced for what seemed like the hundredth time at his watch while they waited. Sims leaned forward as he recalled, "Finally, I passed the word that the next truck to come along was to be the one we would capture."

Only a few minutes passed and Sims saw a motorcyclist, who stopped by the road and went into the courtyard of the house. Sims recalled, "I sent Nicholai to grab him. When Nicholai brought the German back across the road, we discovered this German was sent to check up on the absence of one of our other prisoners, the mail orderly. When he saw the mail orderly beside me, he recognized him as an old friend. The new prisoner calmed down. At least he was near an old friend who had served with him for years."

Sims heard the sound of a truck coming down the road. "We all kneeled down in the darkness beside the roadway. As the truck neared, the German prisoners did as they were ordered and shouted, 'Halt Kamerad'. The truck turned out to be a large five-ton vehicle with a canvas-covered bed on the rear. I ordered Nicholai to check out the back of the truck," Sims smiled, "and Nicholai emerged with fifteen SS troops. More prisoners."

The truck driver was a belligerent German, all but refusing to give up to the Americans. Just short of being abusive, he sat and swore at his dilemma. Sims, through Sergeant Frank, told the driver what was expected of him and that if he did not comply there was to be no leniency. "Reluctantly," Sims said, "the driver obeyed and drove the truck into the small courtyard of the house."

Sims quickly instructed the patrol members to herd out the prisoners from inside the house and load them, along with the fifteen German SS troops, into the rear of the truck, spacing patrol members out in the compartment with loaded Tommy guns to keep them quiet. Sims continued, "I released the civilians and climbed into the cab of the truck with Sergeant Frank, who was to act as interpreter should we encounter Germans on the return trip. The stubborn truck driver used every delaying tactic at his disposal. He purposely flooded out the engine several times. When he stalled the engine several more times I put my .45 pistol near the driver's ear and cocked it to convince him it was in his best interest to operate the truck in a more efficient manner. Grumbling and swearing, the driver again obeyed and we drove off slowly towards Arnhem."

It was October and cold. Cloudy skies and rain trickled down, not in a thunderstorm, but in drizzles and sporadic pulses. Sims had planned on better weather, but was ready to adapt. Luckily, the rain quit as they drove further southeast in the night, passing more trucks and German troops as they went. Patrol members in the rear of the truck were tense, watching their prisoners for the slightest movement towards escape. None would survive if they attempted to jump out. The rear of the covered truck bed had a back flap securely tied to the tailgate section and one patrol member sat at the very rear as a door guard. Cold winds blew under and around the rear flap and both side flaps, chilling the men inside as they bounced down the highway.

The truck stalled out again and the driver kept repeating in German, "This can't be happening to me." Lieutenant Sims and Sergeant Frank sat in the cab, with Sims prodding the driver with the muzzle of his gun. Sims picked up again, "Before the driver could start the engine again, an amphibious jeep pulled up alongside. A German SS officer got out and proceeded to chew out the driver for blocking the road. Canfield jumped from the rear of the truck in a flash and grabbed the officer, dragging him inside the truck bed." They were off again toward Renkum.

Sims said, "I knew we would have to ditch the truck before we reached the river." He considered his options as they rode. By his calculations, he would only use the truck for about ten miles on the highway and then proceed over land on foot. Continuing, Sims quietly spoke, "The original plan was to capture only a couple of prisoners. A six-man patrol could easily guard two or three prisoners back to our lines." Now he was faced with a far more dangerous problem. His prisoners outnumbered his patrol by nearly four to one. If they were detected, he wasn't sure his patrol could survive, not with over twenty prisoners who would surely join any German units who came by.

Sims recalled, "We turned off the main highway and onto a dirt road on the right that led towards a clump of woods barely visible in the dark. The ground turned too soft for the heavy truck. Before we could turn around, the truck was up to the axles, rear tires spinning freely in mud. I knew we were done with the truck, even though Sergeant Frank swore at the driver and had him attempt to free the truck from the mud hole." Climbing to the ground, Sims ordered the prisoners out of the truck. As he exited the rear, the German SS officer took off, thrashing through the undergrowth as he ran into the darkness.

"I didn't need to say a word," Sims said, "but Nicholai bolted after the officer, catching him less than two hundred feet from the truck. We heard Nicholai shoot twice and swear at the officer, calling him an SOB. Becker ran after Nicholai, thinking Nicholai might need help. Becker followed the sound of the commotion and ran up on Nicholai and the officer. Nicholai was still calling the officer an SOB and he kicked him in the seat of the pants. By the time all three returned to the truck, the SS officer was willing and ready to follow orders," Sims smiled.

"It was now after 10:00 pm. In addition, we were running short of time. We needed to be at the river in less than an hour," Sims eyebrows sagged at the remembering. "I gathered the prisoners around and gave them the orders. They were to march in two columns. Our men would be in their midst. If any prisoner made the slightest sound, then we would kill them all. Not one German would survive. I told them it would be just as easy to shoot them as to take them back as prisoners, so they had best follow instructions."

Sims then marched the men, prisoners and all, into the countryside, making no attempt to hide. His belief was that any Germans who saw them marching boldly would think this was just another German troop movement. Nobody would guess that six American paratroopers were taking over twenty Germans prisoner right out in the open. It was a gamble, sure. The German SS officer advised Sims that it wouldn't work. He told Sims, "It is useless to try and cross the Rijn. You might as well turn your weapons over to us because you are sure to be caught." Sims offered, "I didn't answer him or say anything. He asked for a cigarette and I told him I would give him an American cigarette after we crossed the river."

A railway crossing loomed ahead. Sims had originally planned to blow the railway with explosives he had brought along for that purpose. Now, that idea had to be abandoned. Any explosion would attract attention. He did not want to draw any attention from anybody now, especially with all those German prisoners, anyone of whom could shout out at any moment if other German soldiers were near. His predicament was too precarious. Instead, he instructed two patrol members to bury the explosives and then proceed toward the river. That completed, Sims headed the patrol and German prisoners towards Renkum, the nearest village to their crossing point at the river.

Approaching the small village, Sims made another bold choice. Instead of slipping off the road and attempting to sneak to the river, he chose another option. He marched them boldly down the main street, hobnailed boots of the German prisoners making their loud clicking noise on the pavement. Sims grinned, "We heard German voices as we passed through the town, but not one German soldier challenged us or gave us a second look. I guess they thought we were just another unit of marching Germans." They went on through town and headed toward the dike alongside the river, feeling a little giddy at their success. The mood changed as they arrived at the dike.

"A squad of Germans manned a river outpost, in full view of the patrol," Sims said. "I had Sergeant Frank call out in German that there was nothing to worry about as we continued toward the German squad. When we got close, I sent two men to rush the German squad, telling the Germans to put up their hands. We captured those Germans without incident. Two more outposts were captured and those Germans were added to the prisoners." Sims now had 32 German prisoners.

Crouching in the darkness alongside the river, Sims gave the prearranged flashlight signal across the river. The answer came back immediately. Sims spoke calmly, "I sent the German SS officer, truck driver and one patrol member across first. Then I sent prisoners with a patrol member escort across one trip at a time until they were all on the American side."

Major Allen was positioned on the Allied side of the river as the patrol returned. He remembered that November 1st night, "I watched the first boat come ashore.

The German OSS officer kept mumbling something and I finally understood what he was saying. He repeated it over and over, 'this isn't possible, this isn't possible'."

Sims came over in the last boat. When he approached Allen and the German officer, the German SS Officer addressed Sims, "I congratulate you. I didn't believe it was possible."

Sims smiled an acknowledgement and offered the German officer the American cigarette he had promised earlier. The patrol was over.

Each paratrooper of that now famous patrol was awarded the Silver Star. Lieutenant Hugo Sims was awarded the Distinguished Service Cross, invited to a special dinner with General Maxwell Taylor and promoted to the rank of Captain. The story of that one patrol roared through the European theatre, ending up as a feature article in *Life Magazine*. This single patrol put the 101st Airborne at the forefront of the public's eye at a time when great stories were sorely needed at the home front.

The Incredible Patrol made international headlines, but reflection brings about even more admiration as one considers what was accomplished. Sims took his patrol behind enemy lines and stayed there for a night and a day. With crude instruments, Sims navigated six miles deep into German territory in pitch-black darkness, arrived within a hundred feet of his targeted house, and returned with no outside assistance. The patrol was never discovered by any German troops. His patrol did not have one man killed or wounded. In fact, they were never fired upon because of the planning and execution of each detail of the patrol. With the exception of the two warning shots Nicholai fired when the German SS officer attempted to run off, not a shot was fired. The six-man patrol captured and controlled 32 German prisoners in the middle of an entire German Division. Sims was more than pleased that the patrol was a success. Sims recalled, "I was happy that not one man was killed or wounded. That's what sticks with me the most." Incredible might be too weak a word.

Incredible Patrol members

Incredible Patrol members during interview by writer, Cpl. Russ Engel (back towards the camera). Members of the patrol, left to right, were Wilbur, Canfield, Nicolai, Frank, and Becker. Lt. Hugo Sims was not in picture. He was at headquarters getting dental work done at the time of the interview. (Photo courtesy Mark Bando)

**Captured Prisoners during interrogation
after Incredible Patrol**

Captured prisoners were interrogated at the "Slob
Farm", as it was called by the soldiers, at a location
near Zetten, Holland, in late October of 1944.
Lt. Werner Meier (right) did the interrogations.
Waffen-SS Captain Walter Gartner, CO of the *1ˢᵗ
Battalion, SS Artillery Regiment 502* (part of the *ll
SS-Panzer Corps*) is visible on the left in fur collar.
Joe Pangrel, of the 502 Parachute Infantry Regiment
drove up from Dodewaard to view the prisoners and
snapped this photo. (Photo courtesy Mark Bando)

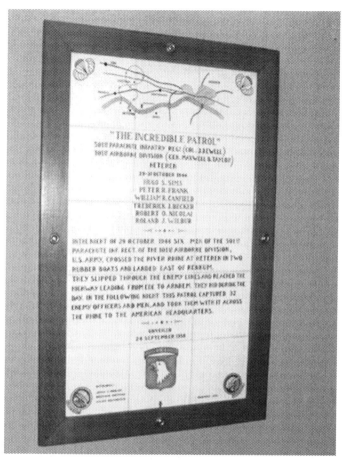

**One of the many plaques and monuments
for "The Incredible Patrol"**

In the town Of Elst, Holland, the Incredible Patrol was honored with this plaque on the inside hallway of the town hall. Hugo Sims and the Patrol were likewise given other monuments and plaques for that famous action. (Photo courtesy Town of Elst, Holland) The plaque reads

"THE INCREDIBLE PATROL

501ˢᵗ PARACHUTE INFANTERY REGt. 9COL. J.J. EWELL)
101ˢᵗ AIRBORNE DIVISION (GEN. MAXWELL D. TAYLOR)

HETEREN 29-31 OCTOBER 1944
HUGO S. SIMS
PETER R. FRANK
WILLIAM R. CANFIELD
FREDERICK J. BECKER
ROBERT O. NICOLAI
ROLAND J. WILBUR

IN THE NIGHT OF 29 OCTOBER 1944 SIX MEN OF THE 501ˢᵗ PARACHUTE INF. REGT. OF THE 101ˢᵗ AIRBORNE DIVISION, U.S. ARMY, CROSSED THE RIVER RHINE AT HETEREN IN TWO RUBBER BOATS AND LANDED EAST OF RENKUM. THEY SLIPPED THROUGH THE ENEMY LINES AND REACHED THE HIGHWAY LEADING FROM EDE TO ARNHEM. THEY HID DURING THE DAY. IN THE FOLLOWING NIGHT THIS PATROL CAPTURED 32 ENEMY OFFICERS AND MEN, AND TOOK THEM WITH IT ACROSS THE RHINE TO THE AMERICAN HEADQUARTERS

UNVEILED 24 SEPTEMBER 1959"

BATTLE OF THE BULGE

BELGIUM

★ ★ ★ ★ ★ ★

Bastogne

"A timid person is frightened before a danger, a coward during the time, and a courageous person afterward."
- John Paul Richter

The Ardennes Mountain range lies in southeastern Belgium, near the intersection of the France-Luxemburg-Belgium borders, a rough-hewn but rolling hill country. Sparsely populated, the elevation and cold winds make for miserable weather during the icy winters. Roads twist back and forth through tight mountain passes and valleys without regard for creature comfort. Local citizens are hearty and hard working, scratching a living from the land and the few resources present. Not much industry takes place in the Ardennes. There is a modest timber industry and some coal mined in the area, but little else of market value. There is not the spectacular beauty of the Alps, but the Ardennes has ample scenery to view if one visits the pristine timber in the high country, or gazes upon the beauty of waterfalls tumbling over solid granite boulders, some the size of large buildings.

In 1944, Bastogne, a rugged town of some 60,000 locals who minded their own business, was perched in the Ardennes mountain range. The town square was surrounded by brick and timber buildings, stone and mortar churches, schools, and an assortment of timber framed houses, barns, and other buildings with slate tile roofing. Railroad tracks ran through town, winding through the Ardennes from Germany to Luxembourg and into Belgium, hauling timber and other raw products from one country to another. Under German control since the early 40's, Bastogne had little ambition except to see the war end. Meanwhile there was nothing the locals could do but endure.

During early December of 1944, Adolph Hitler was confronted by the fact that his army was being steadily pushed back towards the German border by a relentless thrust of Allied forces, a thrust that began with the Normandy invasion and was followed by the Holland campaign. Hitler refused to believe he was losing the war, even though the age of his fighting forces more and more had become young teenagers manning the front lines due to the loss of older, veteran forces of his Third Reich. Many elite Panzer and Grenadier divisions were being decimated and captured at horrendous rates. Replacements and supplies were in high demand, a demand not being met by the German war machine. Hitler had to do something to stem the tide of losses.

As Hitler's forces attempted to stop the Allied progress, nature stepped in. The cold and dreary winter of 1944 saw the Allies' line of advance stagger and stall. The Allies had moved across the continent so quickly they could not keep fuel, ammunition, food and supplies at the front lines. Time and time again convoys pushed overland, scurrying to get supplies to the front. What resulted was the slowing of the march across Belgium. The winter of 1944 saw progress grind to a halt. Allied forces dug in and held the captured lines they had taken in the fall and early winter months. Hitler saw this as his opportunity.

Allied forces had captured and were holding a line that ran north-south from Aachen in the north to a point near the Luxemburg-France intersection, a distance of nearly 90 miles. Hitler boldly planned to pierce the Allied lines and cut off Allied forward units. He could then press the initiative to surround and capture or kill the spearhead of the enemy. If he could pull that off, he could next move to recapture the port at Antwerp and again use the port as the site to re-supply and re-equip his war machine. If successful, he was certain he could change the tide of the war and the Allies would falter and fail. His German supremacy would again rule the continent. All Hitler needed was a successful plan that would cut off and isolate the Allied advance before those elements could receive reinforcement or more supplies and ammunition.

Ambitious though it sounded, even to many German high-ranking commanders, the plan had merit. Hitler planned the operation himself. He presented it to staff officers as an order, an idea, an operation they must execute. Some German high command officers saw the venture as pure folly, a task they had neither manpower nor fuel to support. Without either of these vital resources, they felt, the plan would fail. Hitler neither asked for nor accepted any input from his staff.

The plan was simple. German forces would break through the Allied lines with tanks and heavy artillery fire, followed by a massive infantry attack at critical points in the line presently held by the Allies. Once the breakthrough was completed the infantry was to quickly surround those front line Allied units and destroy them. Hitler studied the latest maps to pinpoint his targets for the initial thrust. If he was to succeed, he needed to capture and control vital roadways and rail facilities to transport German supplies and troops. He would need both to mass transit men and equipment.

One place, one location, had all the elements he needed to sustain his goal. One little Belgium town had rail and highway systems that led directly to his chosen attack route and on to the front, one crossroad town with roads that were almost impossible for an enemy to defend without sustaining unacceptable losses in troops and equipment, one village whose defense was manned by raw recruits being readied for battle and others who were battle weary from hard fighting at the front. Bastogne.

From an Allied military standpoint, Bastogne was an Allied possession, held by the VIII Corps of the First U.S. Army, commanded by General Troy Middleton. The battle to capture Bastogne in the first place had been short and sweet to the victorious Americans. Once Bastogne was firmly in American hands General Middleton moved his VIII Corps command post to the town, using the area surrounding Bastogne as a quick training facility for replacement troops new to the front. Middleton's forces commanded a combat front that extended nearly ninety miles from Aachen near Losheimergraben, Belgium, south to Remich, Luxembourg.

Bastogne was a tired and cold town by December. New Allied infantry arrivals could be moved in and out of this light combat area with the least amount of exposure and risk, while learning the order of battle. Most had arrived less than two weeks earlier fresh from basic training in the States. None had ever heard a shot fired in war. They formed the bulk of the 106th Infantry Division, replacements for the American forces along the Seigfried Line. For all intents, they were still in training. The 106th Infantry occupied a perimeter line outside Bastogne, mostly to the north and east.

Bastogne was also chosen as a close-by area where Allied troops from the front could be sent to rest up for a few days. Some beer drinking and hot food replenished the body. Relief from the constant battle with German forces, even if only for a few days, was R&R for the men. Bastogne was manned in part by the 4th and 28th Infantry Divisions. The 4th was more than 2,000 men under full strength. Both of these combat divisions had been under heavy fighting for sometime and were in the Bastogne area of the Ardennes for badly needed rest. The 9th Armored Division was also at Bastogne, though they too were nowhere near full strength.

Americans and British commanders had moderate tank and artillery batteries staged near Bastogne "just in case"… To the east of town was a semi-circle of small communities, connected by roads running out like spokes of a wheel from Bastogne. These small communities often had fewer than twenty-five houses and were not much more than crossroad junctions. Names like Neffe, Foy, Longvilly, Marvie, Warden, Noville and Bizory would become focal points for Hugo Sims and the 501st.

Before December, those farmland towns and crossroads lived in the shadow of the war more than in a spotlight, and they didn't exist at all in the mind of the young captain who was soon to arrive. Sims' actions in Holland had proved him an excellent officer. His reward, aside from the Distinguished Service Cross, was a promotion to the rank of captain. He was still with Major Richard Allen's command. The two friends were to continue fighting the Germans shoulder-to-shoulder. Each had seen the other in action. Each admired the other. They had solid reason for their mutual respect; they had survived Normandy and Holland. That said it all.

The morning of December 19 brought fog and a damp, misty rain. Typical gripes and groans erupted from the paratroopers as they awoke after a restless sleep. They wanted more sleep. They were tired. They hated cold weather. They hated the Germans. They hated the army. Hated the food. Hated the hurry-up-and-wait. There wasn't much they didn't hate when the gripe sessions started. Gripes and groans were repeated at every opportunity, justified or not. Military men, especially the enlisted corps, acquire the ability to create gripes and groans early in their military life. It wouldn't seem right to not complain. Most knew the complaining was for show. For now, it was time to head out again. Breakfast was a hot meal, for some the last hot meal they would ever taste. For now it was outside for the formation.

The 501st started out of Bastogne behind Colonel Ewell and the First Battalion. Ewell had selected the First as his lead unit. The Second and Third Battalions would follow. As it turned out, the Second and Third followed behind at a great distance. They were bogged down in heavy traffic that grew into one giant traffic jam in Bastogne. Getting those two battalions back into the proper position took another hour. Finally Ewell struck out. It was 0700 hours when Ewell reached the outskirts of Bastogne. His First Battalion formed two columns, one on each side of the road heading east. Some men had no winter coats. A few had no weapon. Still without a rifle, one paratrooper carried a stick, shaking it towards German lines as he walked in the sloppy mud alongside the road. They did not look much like a finely tuned military fighting unit but they were darn sure ready to face anything Hitler could throw their way.

General McAuliffe had given Colonel Ewell the order to move east out of Bastogne, heading towards the town of Longvilly, then continue eastward to a crossroad where the Americans had set up a roadblock four miles past Longvilly. McAuliffe knew the Germans had struck near that location. McAuliffe gave Ewell one order as he pointed at a map, "Move out along this road at 0600, make contact, attack and clear up the situation". What McAuliffe did not know was that 25 divisions of German troops were poised to crash through Allied lines. Ewell was headed straight into their crosshairs.

Of the officers General Middleton and General McAuliffe could have chosen, fate and luck placed precisely the right man for this initial strike in their midst. Six months earlier, Ewell had taken a few days off during a lull in the fighting in Holland. On that busman's holiday, Colonel Julian J. Ewell visited Bastogne to see the landscape. It was a part of the world Ewell wanted to visit. He had no idea he would have the opportunity to pay another visit, especially so soon and certainly not under the conditions he faced that cold morning of December 19. Ewell had walked out of Bastogne on his previous visit to look around. The same roads he walked now were ones he had paced during that visit. Ewell knew the lay of the land, perhaps better than those stationed in Bastogne, and certainly better than any man in the 101st.

Ewell found his knowledge of the terrain valuable that first morning. As his lead element left Bastogne, the point team turned right onto a road heading to the south of their assigned direction of travel. Ewell immediately saw the error. If they continued in that direction, they would not reach the roadblock beyond Longvilly. They would instead be near Marvie, some five miles further south and west of their objective. Ewell ran to the intersection where the wrong turn had occurred. Most of the point element was already out of sight on the winding road. Ewell stopped the men and corrected their direction, then set out on the correct road. The point platoon had to backtrack to the intersection at a trot. They passed the men in the column to retake their position at the head of the column.

Farmland and swaying hogback hills surround Bastogne. It has been mistaken in the minds of outsiders as a quaint little village high in the mountain ranges. In reality, it is situated more in an undulating set of valleys and foothills. Photographs of the area surrounding Bastogne show neatly carved farms with contoured planted fields and pastures. Hills around Bastogne shield many areas from view. Twisting roads and sharp drop-offs are present in abundance. Tight cutbacks and thick woods appear throughout the area. Trees are old timber, thick and high, filtering out sunlight under the canopies in summer. In some places the roads are completely hidden under evergreens during winter. Some exposed roads wander through valley floors, in full sight from surrounding hills and swales.

Bastogne provided good cover and concealment for men and equipment to move about without being seen by an enemy. German forces massed east of Bastogne were well concealed. Artillery, tanks and infantry moved about with ease. American forces were stretched too thin to gather accurate intelligence. As a result, Hitler's plan was unfolding as planned. German tanks moved into position to prepare for their artillery barrages. Infantry units staged behind the tanks and mobile artillery. Hitler's initial strike routed American troops east of Bastogne, forcing them into a retreat towards Bastogne. General Middleton did not have adequate resources to reinforce the hard hit line out towards Longvilly.

Colonel Ewell did not know the American roadblock at his targeted crossroad was already cut off and surrounded. The few who could escape did so to the west through woods and fields back towards the safety of Bastogne. As Ewell met the retreating forces, they appeared to be in shock and wandering around aimlessly. When Ewell questioned some as they arrived, he gathered no useful information. Some men stared back with a blank gaze. Others had left the front line so quickly their scant information was fragmented and without substance. Ewell made no further attempt to stop others in the retreating lines, and he quit asking questions of the exhausted and worn troops. He would rely on his own intelligence team. He had no other viable options.

Ewell's men did approach stragglers and asked for weapons and whatever ammunition they carried. Those retreating soldiers quickly handed over everything the paratroopers wanted. They were through with the fight. They were going back to the rear. They did not need nor want rifles or ammunition.

Five thousand yards out of Bastogne on the Longvilly road was the small threadbare town of Neffe. The road ran southwest to northeast through the hamlet from Bastogne to Longvilly and on into Luxemburg and Germany. A railroad paralleled the roadway some fifty yards south of the main road. Two other roads intersected at Neffe, one to Bizory on the north side and one towards Marvie and Wardin on the south of Neffe.

An American roadblock was set at the intersection of the Neffe-Bizory roads on the outskirts of the tiny village of Neffe. It was under sporadic artillery fire from German mobile light artillery. High-pitched rounds screeched in at regular intervals, tossing shrapnel in the roadblock. American troops could only sit tight and hope for the best. They had no way of knowing where the rounds came from and they could see nothing in their sight lines.

A small river, more like a creek with steep banks than a flowing river, ran along the south side of the road between the railroad and the roadway. On the other side of the road were sloping hills rising up towards the north. Morning fog hung low in the valley and visibility was less than 500 yards. Colonel Ewell went over the terrain in his mind; details still fresh from his fall visit. The road straightened out for seven hundred yards before entering Neffe. There was scant protection from German artillery or machine gun fire in such open terrain. The command group that included Ewell and his staff, followed his First Battalion point platoon. The damp mist collected on the paratroopers as they cautiously plodded towards their objective. There was no room to maneuver on the south side of the road and only open ground to the left. Ewell proceeded with caution.

The Second and Third Battalions of the 501st were still in Bastogne. Ewell wanted reinforcements if needed in a hurry and sent for them both. The heavy fog restricted any view of his front or flanks. Ewell wanted to beef up his presence east of Bastogne and have a formidable combat force in case the German troops outnumbered his forces. Bringing up the two battalions gave him options if a German attack developed.

Both battalions in Bastogne were caught in another gigantic traffic jam with Middleton's VIII Corps clogging the streets, in full evacuation. Every street intersection was a jumble of stopped men and vehicles with long lines of men, trucks, jeeps, tanks and every other vehicle in VIII Corps' fleet waiting to move. Both battalions attempted other city streets only to find the traffic congestion citywide. There would be no swift help from either of Ewell's battalions in Bastogne.

Hugo Sims was out front with Ewell's forces. What intelligence he had was no better than that of Ewell. Sims could offer no new information about what lurked beyond the fog. German forces were hitting the front lines in several places to the east. Sims recalled, "Our largest concern was that the Germans had more men and tanks than expected. If paratroopers faced an equal number of Germans, the level of concern was far less than if the Germans were massed in large numbers to attack with tanks and artillery in support. All the information we had was hearsay and rumors, hardly information to be trusted."

Before the Second and Third Battalions got out of Bastogne, Ewell and his First Battalion were raked by German machine gun fire. Paratroopers hit the ground, seeking whatever cover was nearby. Some scrambled down the creek bank; others dove onto the left shoulder of the road where there was a shallow depression. Paratroopers up front returned fire, but they were shooting for effect, not at identifiable targets. They could see no sign of the machine gun in the fog. Ewell decided to lay low and wait to see if a German attack was to follow.

The German machine gun went silent. The First Battalion grew tense. If the Germans were set to attack, any second now they would charge. All eyes bore down on the fog bank. Fingers flipped off safeties. Cigarettes were tossed aside. Stomachs tightened. Tension mounted. Nothing moved out front. Had the Germans retreated? Were they dug in up there, waiting for the paratroopers to attack? Ewell knew the area. Waiting was his best option.

Sims remembered the incident vividly, "No heavy vehicle sounds came from out front. If the Germans had tanks to attack, those tanks would make a loud and clanking noise as they moved. We knew the Germans had tanks in the area but there was no way of knowing where those tanks were or where they were heading."

Commander of the First Battalion was Major Raymond V. Bottomly, Jr., a proven and experienced combat officer. As Ewell jockeyed for more information and pondered his next move, Bottomly had his men of the First Battalion spread out and dug in. Ewell moved back one hundred yards behind the skirmish line of the First and set up a command post in a tight little hollow just past a turn in the road inside a stone cottage. Bottomly, veteran of Normandy and Holland, saw his position as unstable at best. One artillery element of the 907th Glider Field Artillery Battalion under Lt. Colonel Clarence F. Nelson sped toward Ewell's and Bottomly's positions. Bottomly heard the radio traffic and was relieved to hear support was on the way.

Lt. Colonel Nelson had some anxious moments about his artillery capability. Five of his guns had never been fired and the radios had not been tested. He decided to proceed anyway. Setting up his guns a thousand yards behind Bottomly's line, Captain Gerald J. McGlone, commanding officer of B Battery, 907th, commenced firing. He directed fire up and over Bottomly's First Battalion towards Neffe, into the fog. Lt. Colonel Nelson was satisfied the one battery was enough and waited for further orders from Ewell.

The artillery support was precisely what Ewell needed. The Germans facing Bottomly did not attack. Ewell was convinced the artillery support had shown the Germans his paratroopers had heavy weapon support if the Germans attacked. Either Ewell was correct or German commanders had other plans. It appeared a stalemate had been reached. Neither side advanced and neither side pulled back. Generals McAuliffe and Middleton, back in Bastogne, felt a measure of relief since Ewell had drawn a line in the sand and held the Germans at bay.

Though Ewell and Bottomly held a line facing east, both knew their left flank towards Bizory was in jeopardy. They had no support on that side and no men to deploy in that direction. The Germans fired several more artillery rounds into the First Battalion area, causing no death or injuries to the paratroopers. Still, their presence sent danger signals to Ewell. He realized he could not attack into Neffe. German tanks were sure to be there and the artillery fire appeared to be coming from his left front, across the open fields, perhaps from crests of the small hills towards Bizory. Any attempt to move the First Battalion forward would fail.

With Germans controlling the valley Ewell would have to deal with the tanks and artillery first. As Ewell stood facing Neffe, with Bastogne at his back, Bizory was to his left front, less than two thousand yards north of Neffe. The landscape rose gradually from Neffe towards Bizory. The crests of the hills towards Bizory offered ideal firing lines into Neffe and the lower land surrounding the hills. The hills between the two villages provided ample views to target accurate supporting artillery and tank fire.

A talented and skilled tactician, Ewell rapidly developed a plan of action.

Ewell sent the Second and Third Battalions out east of Bastogne. The Second had staged in an assembly point only two hundred yards outside Bastogne. Ewell ordered the Second Battalion, under command of Major Sammie N. Homan, to seize Bizory and establish a skirmish line to link up with Bottomly. It was an ambitious plan but Ewell had to establish a secure left flank if he was to remain in control of the valley.

The Second Battalion hurriedly went into action. Major Homan sent all his battalion into the attack plan, pulsing forward. His battalion encountered stiff resistance several times. At each German strongpoint the Germans fired a filicide of machine gun fire and some mortars, then retreated. As they retreated, Homan advanced toward the tiny hamlet. Moving squads one at a time in typical fire and maneuver tactics, his progress did not waiver. Bizory was in Allied hands before 1300 hours.

Ewell's actions took on new significance. The Germans were in an all-out assault to break through the American lines. Up to this point, they had encountered one success after another. Ewell, after taking Bizory, moved on to take the crests of the hills where German mobile artillery was located. He then completed the linkup between Bottomly's First Battalion and Homan's Second Battalion, thus providing him a skirmish line filled with veteran paratroopers that stretched from Bizory to Neffe. Ewell next sent the Third Battalion, under Lt. Colonel George M. Griswold, to the south of Neffe towards Mont, a scant fifteen hundred yards southwest. This would extend his skirmish line beyond Neffe in case the Germans used that area to attempt an attack from his right flank.

Ewell's actions turned out to have profound implications. German commanders east of Bastogne were poised to overrun Bastogne and put the American infantry in a retreat. With Ewell's deployment of the 501st in position as an offensive line, any German thrusts would encounter paratroopers attacking them in an organized combat formation across a wide front. Such an action was exactly opposite from what the Germans expected. Tactics appeared to have changed in mid-battle.

Before this maneuver, the Americans had put up return fire to cover a retreat as they left. Not this time. The German attack stalled and once they stopped the attack the paratroopers gained spirit and enthusiasm. The Germans then fell back. This was not how it was planned. German commanders could not regain the initiative. Ewell's tactic served both to stop the Germans and to make them believe a major Allied offensive was forthcoming.

Colonel Ewell had set out with orders to control the east side of Bastogne and take the attack to the Germans. He followed those orders until they could not be completed. What followed was ultimately the final blueprint for the brilliant defense of Bastogne. Ewell's skirmish line defense retreated toward Bastogne as the Germans threw more men, artillery and tanks into the battle. Though retreating, the Allies never gave in to panic and never allowed German forces to penetrate the inner ring of defense. The pattern for the defense of Bastogne was not yet finished but the die was cast.

Generals McAuliffe and Middleton did not know they were facing an enemy that outnumbered their own forces by four to one, not until the fight was over.

General Middleton, on December 18th, established an initial plan to ward off German offensive attacks. His original plan was to send men out to the outlying areas of Bastogne to engage the enemy and set up defensive positions against any German attack. This would provide a strong buffer zone in which Middleton could move about as the situation developed.

Colonel William L. Roberts was the commander of Combat Command B, 10th Armored Division. Having been one of the earliest units to arrive in Bastogne, Roberts met with General Middleton to receive his orders. Middleton did not hesitate in asking, "How many teams can you make up?"

Roberts replied, "Three."

Middleton gave him specifics. "One team will go to the southeast of Wardin, one team to the vicinity of Longvilly and one team to the vicinity of Noville."

Roberts broke down his unit into three teams, Team Cherry, Team O'Hara and Team Desobry. He gave Team Cherry, under Lt. Colonel Henry Cherry, the Longvilly assignment to the east. Team O'Hara, under Lt. Colonel James O'Hara, went towards Wardin on the southeast. Team Desobry, under Major William Desobry drew the northern route towards Noville. Each team would face torrid fighting in the coming days but the worst may have been the northern road at Noville.

Team Cherry moved east toward Longvilly. Lt. Colonel Cherry had elements of the 20th Armored

Infantry Battalion, the 55th Engineer battalion and units of the 90th Cavalry Squadron attached to his force. Team Cherry never reached Longvilly. Just west of the town they were stalled by stiff German offensive. By midnight on the 18th, Team Cherry was the lone defender of Longvilly. Before daylight Team Cherry was cut off and surrounded. The morning was filled with fierce fighting to withdraw Team Cherry and the action was completed in the early afternoon when Lt. Colonel Cherry broke through at Mageret. It was decided that Team Cherry could not contain the German offensive and all its energy went into covering the flanks and moving back towards Bastogne.

Team O'Hara had no better success in controlling the southeast towards Wardin. At first the situation appeared stable. Lt. Colonel O'Hara set up his command post on a small rise just outside a patch of woods on the southwest of Wardin. From that location he could observe the town and monitor any activity. Morning fog was dense and heavy on the 19th. Wardin lay somewhere inside the thick fog and visibility was less than a hundred yards. O'Hara waited for the fog to lift, confident that no German attack was imminent. O'Hara sent two men to check out Wardin. They returned after being fired on in the town and reported that Germans were already in the village.

Near noon the fog lifted somewhat. Visibility was close to eight hundred yards. Company I of the 501st approached Wardin from the northeast. Team O'Hara could see Germans approaching the village in small groups, but the Germans were passing through gullies and the reverse side of small land rises and O'Hara could not bring them under fire. Artillery in Bastogne was too involved in other firing missions to provide help.

What followed was disaster. Company I was caught in Wardin by a German battalion filled with tank and mobile artillery. Captain Wallace, commanding officer of I Company, misread or did not know about German strengths in Wardin. Before help could arrive his company was being hammered back down the street towards Bastogne. They fought back to cover the retreat. Company I was decimated. Final numbers showed Company I had entered Wardin with two hundred men. After the Company returned to Bastogne only eighty-three survived. Captain Wallace and three other officers died in the fight at Wardin. For all intents and purposes Company I ceased to exist as a fighting unit.

Team Desobry went north towards Noville on the 18th. The time was just before midnight when the team assembled at Noville. Major Desobry set up a tank position at each of the three roads running north and northwest out of Noville. During the night two of the three had already been attacked but had driven back the Germans.

Just after daylight on the 19th, Desobry brought all three teams back into his position near Noville. Fog lay like a blanket across the meadows and hung low to the ground. Visibility here was no better than it was for Team O'Hara or Team Cherry on the other side of Bastogne. Desobry held his ground as he waited in the drifting fog.

Just after 8:30 two German Tiger tanks emerged from the fog on the north side of Noville. Team Desobry destroyed both. By midmorning the fog was burning off and Team Desobry saw Germans approaching with a full complement of armored units, tanks and mobile artillery. A fierce battle raged on and by its conclusion, Desobry's men had knocked out ten of the fourteen tanks. By noon the entire countryside in view was littered with dead Germans as well as disabled and burning tanks. The lull was temporary.

Germans were on three sides of Team Desobry. They were in danger of being cut off. Colonel Roberts radioed that a battalion was in route to help. Desobry readied for a counterattack. Colonel Roberts sent in Lt. Colonel James LaPrade and his First Battalion of the 506th PIR. The two unit commanders worked together and persisted through the day, but they neither gained nor lost ground. Artillery from each side pounded the other.

Late in the afternoon the fog returned, drifting slowly down from the hilltops. Desobry and LaPrade shared command of the combined unit at Noville. Throughout the day the fight continued. High ground was a critical issue to both Desobry and LaPrade. They sent three companies assisted with tanks out to capture the high ground, but as the day passed into late afternoon fog reappeared. With vision impaired and German artillery injuring many soldiers, both officers agreed to pull the remainder of the three companies back into Noville.

General Higgins, the 101st Division Assistant Commander, arrived at Noville. A discussion with LaPrade and Desobry followed. It was agreed that LaPrade was senior in rank and should assume command of the combined forces at Noville. Less than an hour later, tragedy struck. A shell from a German 88 landed near the command post, killing LaPrade and wounding

Desobry. Newly arrived Major Robert Harwick assumed command.

Back in Bastogne, Generals McAuliffe and Middleton could see that German forces on the north were well equipped and backed by strong armor. The north side would continue to weaken under heavy German attacks. Within another two days the American forces would give up Noville and shift back to Foy as their defensive line.

December 20th saw more than just weather changes when snow arrived. Morale was dampened by the constant pulling back of forces, but the attitude of the paratroopers remained resolute. None believed the Germans could defeat them. Most viewed the tightening of the circle around Bastogne as nothing more than a re-posturing to hold the upper hand.

Captain Hugo Sims was as determined as the other paratroopers in Bastogne, "The weather was miserable. Food and supplies dwindled. German artillery and mortars dropped on us at random and when the cold rain quit on the 20th, snows came and the temperature plunged. When it started to snow, it came down in large flakes. Before noon it was several inches deep and starting to cover everything. It was pretty at first, but then the really cold wind came in and it wasn't pretty very long. It was cold, too cold for this southern boy."

Staying warm became an hourly fight of its own. Nobody escaped. A somber mood arrived, as did blankets of powdery snow. A scenic winter wonderland landscape was steadily being displaced with exploding tree-bursts of German heavy weapons fire during the dreary days and cold nights. Letters home were not written. Everyone knew the mail wasn't going to get out. Christmas was coming and the paratroopers felt sure Santa would detour around Bastogne.

Paratroopers and officers in Bastogne found little in the way of creature comforts. Sims appeared to shiver in remembrance of the bitter cold, "Some may have enjoyed limited time under a roof, but fuel for fires was scarce. Inside most stone and timber buildings was nearly as cold as outside temperatures. Broken timbers from destroyed buildings became our prime fuel targets, as did the few scant coal supplies we could find. It was a time of low food supplies and even lower stocks of ammunition."

Sims bore his job as an intelligence officer without the resources he needed, "Communications with units outside Bastogne were by wire telephone. Those wires were routinely cut by German artillery round explosions as well as the intentional cutting of those lines by German troops." Sims was to find himself in another job before the Bastogne fight was over but until that happened, he continued to move between headquarters in the town and the front lines, gathering and dispensing intelligence about German forces and their movements.

Sims saw that overall morale remained high even though somber moods surfaced. Upon reflection, his words were, "Bastogne was not really unusual as far as we saw it. We were pretty much isolated on all our missions. We parachuted ahead of our forces every time we jumped. We were used to being under fire and dealing with the problems we faced on our own. We never gave it a lot of thought. We were trained to be self-sufficient so there wasn't really anything new about our situation in Bastogne. We never thought the Germans could take Bastogne from us. I just wished we had more food and ammo that first week... and some warmer clothes."

Major Richard Allen shared the same sentiment, "Every time we jumped we were behind enemy lines. We were trained to be surrounded."

Nothing came easy when the snows arrived. That first snow came down in massive flakes, covering the ground with over eight inches of thick snow the first four hours. The ground was already wet from earlier rain, creating slippery and sloppy footholds everywhere. Foxholes were still to be dug and the cold ground did not give in easily. Sometimes four men would share a foxhole but most of the time it was just two. They shared what few blankets were available to keep warm.

At night the temperature dropped below 15 degrees and even made it down near zero one night. When it got that cold men huddled close together under blankets. Sims recalled the conditions well, "Logs and tree limbs were placed over foxholes, then covered with a piece of canvas or parachute canopy, anything to keep out that cold wind and snow. Tree limbs sagged under the fluffy snow cover. Tanks were nearly invisible until they moved and the snow fell off. Walking was difficult." The scenery was picture postcard quality until the explosions of war interrupted.

A fire in a foxhole gave away a location to any German with a decent pair of binoculars, providing a good target for artillery, especially at night. Orders proclaimed no fires were to be lit but paratroopers got so cold they chanced small fires during daylight with brightly burning dry small tree limbs that gave off little smoke. Feet and hands were thrust near the flames. Warmth was temporary and limited to one side of a hand or foot but even that little feeling of heat was a luxury. Socks and gloves placed around the fire felt toasty when placed back on cold and wet hands or feet. The memory was vivid as Sims spoke, "We knew the fires were forbidden, but most front line officers overlooked small fires."

Huddled down deep in foxholes for warmth, troops ate what was available: K-rations, brittle chocolate bars, and whatever they could salvage or get from other troops. Men scooped snow into canteen cups to heat water on the fires for hot chocolate and instant coffee. Hot meals from the cooks showed up more than expected and they eagerly wolfed it down each time. Still, it was never enough and hunger pangs remained. Food shortages were becoming a major concern.

The KP staff set up shop in an abandoned school building in Bastogne. They cooked and served food on makeshift tables. Cooks carried hot food out to the lines when possible. In an atmosphere where everything was freezing cold, a hot meal warmed more than just stomachs. Often that food trip was futile. German artillery and tank rounds plastered the trees and front line positions steadily, and tree bursts often-blasted limbs and debris down on food before it could be eaten on the front lines. Still, the cooks never stopped making the trips.

One food item became a staple. A paratrooper was searching houses and buildings when he discovered a hollow wall concealing a storehouse of flour and sugar. Cooks quickly mastered a pancake recipe and made sugary syrup for the wounded. They soon expanded the process to provide pancakes to as many paratroopers as possible. Hot pancakes became steady fare, especially for the wounded. Pancakes with watery sweet syrup were filling. Several paratroopers vowed they would never again eat a pancake in their life. It reminded them too much of those freezing days and bloody nights under siege that cold winter in Bastogne.

Some animals became meals. Cattle and oxen became a meal for some. When an artillery round or stray bullet killed an animal, cooks set out to butcher the animals. Sims saw the actions of the cooks, "They were not experts at skinning and butchering but they learned real fast. An ox fed many men, so did a cow. Seasoning was scarce but that didn't matter. It was food. It was meat and it was hot. We were all were grateful for that."

Cooks set up several other kitchens in underground cellars and storage rooms. Their cook stoves were in full use. Appetites for hot food kept them busy twenty-four hours a day. Menus were limited and seasonings lacking but it was hot food. Paratroopers stated weak obligatory grumbles and gripes while knowing they were getting the best food available under the worst conditions possible. Respect for the cooks swelled each time a man in the front line tasted hot food.

Overcast skies and low clouds kept Bastogne sealed off from re-supply by air. Each day anxious faces turned skyward, hoping to see Allied aircraft bringing supplies. Day after day nothing changed. Planes could fly over the top of those thick clouds, but they couldn't drop supplies where they couldn't see. Heavy snows continued dumping thick blankets on Bastogne as Allied high command realized Bastogne was in serious trouble of being cut off and surrounded.

Ammunition was running dangerously low. Mortars and automatic weapon rounds were so scare that small unit use was severely impaired. Sharing became the order of the day. Artillery units were rationed to ten rounds per gun per day with no gun firing more than four rounds unless directed by their commanding officer. An added requirement was that a target had to be observed before artillery could be fired. No more blanketing of a suspected German stronghold or position. This caused a ripple of fear in some front line units. Suppose they were under attack but couldn't see the attackers' heavy tanks and artillery. Could they expect help? Should they fire off their daily ration of rounds?

Artillery and mortar rounds were not the only ammunition shortages. Men on the front lines were rationing their rounds, too. All the skirmishes and firefights had drained their ammunition supplies. Some had already resorted to using captured German rifles and ammunition. One man had two extra clips of ammunition for his M-1, only two. With one clip in the rifle and those two clips, he had a total of 24 bullets. He went from one foxhole to another in an attempt to find ammo. He returned with three hand grenades, a captured German bolt action rifle, and 13 rounds of ammunition for it. Any strong German attack and he might end up in a bayonet and hand-to-hand battle to survive.

To make matters worse, the medical situation deteriorated early in the fight and did not improve until help arrived in Bastogne. On December 19, an attempt was made to relocate the medical surgery unit to a crossroad on the western outskirts of Bastogne. Lt. Colonel David Gold, the surgeon of the 101st, and Lt. Carl W. Coles, division supply officer, made the decision to relocate, believing that to be a safer location for the division hospital. German forces attacked and captured the bulk of the regimental surgeons and medical supplies for Bastogne before midnight. The loss of the medical staff crippled medical efforts. Not only were they now without vital surgeons but they had few medical supplies. The remaining medical forces in Bastogne had critical shortages that affected the quality of the care they could render to wounded Allied troops.

Surgeons in Bastogne set up new locations and revised procedures for handling wounded troopers. They needed a building with more space. Wounded were coming in so fast there was no place to put them. The critically wounded who needed surgery would be placed in a large church sanctuary where surgeons worked under candlelight 24 hours a day. Less critically wounded were moved to a nearby school to be cared for by medics taking turns day and night. Those wounded that would not survive were placed against one wall of the large chapel on beds of straw and covered with the few blankets scrounged by medics. Sims recalled the grim scene, "As one man died, he was taken outside and his body placed alongside other dead soldiers, his blanket taken and used on other wounded men inside. The stack of bodies outside kept growing."

A gaping hole in the roof of the chapel allowed snow flurries to drift through the sanctuary. Cold wind swirled in the open chapel. Medics gave up their coats to cover wounded men. Artillery shells continued to rain in on Bastogne. German fighter-bombers poured a steady dose of quick strikes on the town, strafing any target of opportunity then dropping their bombs before disappearing into heavy clouds. Air strikes caused debris and shrapnel to contaminate the surgery area but there was nothing the doctors could do to alter that situation. They kept working to save as many lives as possible.

Surgeons in Bastogne that cold December knew they were losing men they could save if those men could be relocated to a surgery unit with more equipment and doctors. Doctors and surgeons were forced into a triage decision none wanted. They made the hard decision to let some men die purely because they had no other options. Neither the medical supplies, equipment, nor surgical expertise were at hand to keep them alive. Dying troops along the sidewall of the chapel were under the watchful eye of a medic who comforted them as best he could.

Morphine was dangerously below necessary levels. Wounded men suffered great pain but nothing could be done to help without supplies. There were too many wounded men and too few doctors. Morphine and whole blood were used only sparingly where it was an absolute necessity. There wasn't enough to go around and no one knew when to expect re-supply.

Two thousand yards north of Bastogne on the Houffalize road was the hamlet of Noville. The crossroad at Noville was to be captured and held by the 506th PIR of the 101st Division. A vicious battle for Noville ensued. Germans pushed back the paratroopers in one savage attack then lost Noville back to the Americans. Noville became typical of the many small village firefights that characterized the battlefield in the Ardennes. Experienced German units faced off against the 101st in a land tug-of-war, only to see the American forces pull back into a tighter circle around Bastogne. Noville was finally lost to the Germans after three fierce battles.

As December 20th came to an end, so did American use of the only road in or out of Bastogne, cut off and controlled by German tanks and troops. Germans held the ground on all four sides. Bastogne was closed to any Allied forces outside the perimeter set up by the 101st. No friendly forces were expected to arrive quickly enough to save Bastogne. The American forces in Bastogne were sealed off from the outside world. The defenders in Bastogne were alone.

By December 21, German units controlled Noville on the north, Bizory, Neffe, Mont, Wardin and Marvie on the east, Villeroux and Assenois on the south, and Longchamps, Bertogne and Mande St. Etienne on the west. In Bastogne, Colonel Kinnard advised high command by radio when asked for a situation report, "Picture a doughnut. We're the hole".

A glaring weakness of the Americans was a lack of major artillery support fire. The Americans were fortunate that the Germans did not know about this weakness. In a brilliant tactical move, Kinnard suggested and McAuliffe agreed to place artillery in the center of the surrounded forces. When German forces attacked from any one side, artillery would be rushed to that side of the circle and direct concentrated fire upon the attackers. As quickly as the Germans were thrown back the artillery units reassembled in the center of the 'doughnut hole'. This tactic worked so well that German forces concluded there was a vast American artillery element in Bastogne that the Germans had not known about all along.

The shifting back and forth of artillery to support the perimeter defense of Bastogne was an example of swift utilization of available resources. However, artillery could support only one directional support mission at a time. If the Germans had attacked from more than one direction at the same time, the story of Bastogne may have had a different outcome.

December 21 brought more snow and incoming German artillery fire. German fighter planes swooped down to strafe and bomb. Bombs killed indiscriminately, including many locals who had not been fortunate enough to escape before Bastogne became the hole in the doughnut. Their bodies lay where they died in the fields and streets, sometimes in and under the rubble of houses and buildings. A nun who stayed to help care for the wounded was fatally wounded by a blast that destroyed part of the chapel being used as a hospital. There was no escape from Bastogne by then. The life of every living soul in Bastogne hung on the ability of the American defenders to hold the town.

"It didn't even look like the same town we entered a few days earlier," Sims recalled. "Buildings had no roofs and some had fallen in on whoever lived there. There were bodies in the rubble. Bombing and artillery barrages took a pretty heavy toll. Tanks, Jeeps and equipment trailers swerved around high piles of stone, bricks and debris to drive across the town. Some streets didn't look like streets with all the collapsed buildings. Snow covered the piles, adding new white lumps that weren't there before."

Some buildings had only a wall or two still starkly pointing to the sky. Broken and shattered furniture was strewn about in the rubble and out onto curbs and streets. Gaping holes from bombs exploding squarely in the middle of the stone and rock roadways of the city became crater-like obstacles. Vehicles hit by incoming rounds remained as burned out hulks of twisted metal.

Sims spoke about the artillery constantly fired by the Germans at the 101st during the struggle in Bastogne. "German artillery was coming in day and night. I don't know if the rounds were above ground detonating rounds or whether the rounds struck trees, which would then detonate the shell. We tried to stay underground in foxholes during the shelling. Men used fallen limbs and logs to cover the foxholes, draping any material they could find, like parachute canopies or bed sheets, over the limbs and logs. Then they would lay another layer of logs crossways over the first one and pile straw or anything they could scrounge up to make the foxhole roof a little stronger in protecting them from the artillery blasts."

Sims remembered the scene, "Tree limbs and huge splinters blasted off trees were almost as lethal as the shrapnel from the shells. When exploded by an incoming round, the tree limbs and chunks of wood flew out and down on the men. That's why they worked so hard to build up a roof over the foxhole. It wouldn't stop a direct hit, but wood splinters and small tree limbs couldn't penetrate the roof. Men would leave a narrow slit at the ground line for firing holes. Snow piled up and covered the foxholes so they looked like lumps or small snow mounds in the woods. It was so cold, the foxholes became a home for small fires of dry wood and sticks to help warm hands and feet."

About the cold, Sims commented, "Everybody was cold. You've got to remember we didn't have the best of winter clothing. Boots were just leather, no insulation. Socks were standard issue, as were the clothes, with not much insulation. The routine, which became necessary to keep warm was to put on layer after layer of clothes, then cover up with whatever was around. The dead soldiers became a source of clothes for the living. It was all we had. There were no stores left in Bastogne where we could get clothing. We even used tarps from the trucks as insulation and as blankets. When it got down to near zero, men did whatever they could do just to make it through another night. I was lucky. I was moving between the front lines and headquarters most of the time. Moving around so much helped the circulation. Those men down in foxholes had to rub their feet and hands for circulation. There wasn't much else they could do to keep warm, except for those small fires. They had to keep undercover."

Evening was a dim and lonely sight. A few candles and kerosene lanterns glittered behind some windows and doorways but for the most part the city was dark and foreboding at night. American troops hurried from one building to another to check on a report or pass on information just received from the communication detachment, their shadowy figures often bent at the waist as they moved about the town. Officers huddled around makeshift tables to review maps and daily progress reports. Snow flurries rambled through open roofed structures in cold swirls. Men looking up could see the black cloudy skies without obstruction.

Civilian traffic was reduced to walking and horse-and-cart vehicles carrying what remained of meager possessions, not that there were a high number of locals remaining in Bastogne. Many civilians were from outlying farming communities and crossroad villages making their way to the west to get away from the voracious fighting. They scurried to get out of town as quickly as possible. Children tagged along on foot, clothing worn but warm. Tight stocking caps and mittens adorned tiny heads and hands. They walked staring around in bewilderment at the sight of Bastogne. They certainly did not remember it this way. Food was scarce and they looked as though they had missed many meals.

General Middleton knew he watched people who were as hungry and tired as the Americans entrenched to fight the Germans. His men were hungry too. Feeding the civilians was something he could not do. No supplies could get into Bastogne. Paratroopers did share food, but only meager amounts were on hand. One family walked beside their horse driven cart, a father, mother and six children, looking back over their shoulder as an American photographer snapped their picture. Middleton could only do so much with so little. His primary duty was to defend Bastogne. All else would stand in line.

Middleton constantly radioed an urgent request for ammunition, food, winter clothing and medical supplies. His request did not fall on deaf ears but heavy cloud cover precluded airdrops for miles around Bastogne. Allied high command understood the need and they were ready to fly in those supplies at the first break in the weather. Middleton was by then pacing the command post, a deep concern that if ammunition and supplies did not arrive before long he would not be able to maintain his position.

Staff officers and personnel had already given their coats to units on the front line. Any ammunition they could find had been passed out. Stockpiles were all but nonexistent. All the determination to hold Bastogne would evaporate without ammunition. Barehanded men couldn't win against German tanks. Middleton knew help was on the way if Patton could break through, but if he didn't get through soon and no supplies got in, Middleton knew full well that Bastogne would fall to the Germans. He had to prepare for any eventuality, and he was not going to surrender the town.

No day in Bastogne stood out in Hugo Sims' mind like December 23rd. "We saw blue sky. About 9:00 the first C-47s dropped pathfinders with radar units to designate the drop zone. There must have been twelve or fifteen planes in that first flight. In minutes there were American silver fighter planes diving at German positions, strafing and bombing. They came in small groups and attacked German positions all around Bastogne." No German planes arrived to confront the fighter planes as they streaked downward at high speed toward a target. Pilots pulled back hard on the stick and the sleek plane bottomed out and climbed upward to complete an arc in the sky. A moment later a dark cloud of smoke rose from the ground followed by the sound of the explosion of the bomb released by the pilot.

Targets for the fighter-bombers were called up to the pilots by radio. Once alerted to a specific location where Germans were massed, the pilot swooped down in a surprise attack. In the four-day window of clear weather, more than 250 sorties were flown against the Germans. Heavy snow left tracks from German tanks that led into wooded areas. Pilots followed those tracks and bombed the woods, destroying many tanks and artillery positions where they lay hidden, or so they thought, deep in the trees.

"In late morning, sometime before noon," Sims remembered, "we saw more C-47s coming. There were hundreds of them parachuting pallets of supplies on one large field not far from division headquarters. There was lots of activity around the big field. Some of the men cheered. Everyone watched and waited. We couldn't go out and get the supplies until the planes finished the drop but that was some sight to see. We had jeeps with trailers around the drop zone just waiting to get the pallets when the drop was over."

Over two hundred and forty planes dropped supplies to Bastogne that day. The pilots held a steady course over the drop zone in formations as they had in the Holland campaign. Over fourteen hundred parachutes filled the sky. In a steady line the C-47s converged on the open field to deliver life-saving supplies. Sims recalled, "I just sat and smiled. That was some sight."

Men used more than just the contents of the pallets. They used burlap bags that contained bundles of K-rations as wrapping to warm feet. Parachutes became blankets and foxhole covers. Spirits rose as load after load of ammunition was dispersed to men on the front line. Artillery officers smiled. Rationing was over. Christmas was still two days off but presents arrived that clear and cold morning on December 23.

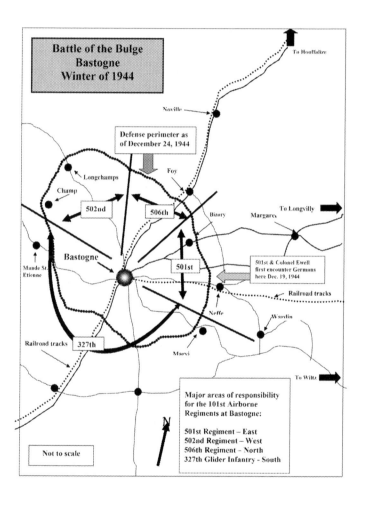

Battle of the Bulge
Bastogne
Winter of 1944

To Houffalize

Noville

Defense perimeter as
of December 24, 1944

Foy

Longchamps

Champ

502nd

506th

Bizory

Margaret

To Longvilly

Maude St.
Etienne

Bastogne

501st

501st & Colonel Ewell
first encounter Germans
here Dec. 19, 1944

Railroad tracks

Neffe

Wardin

Railroad tracks

327th

Marvi

To Wiltz

Major areas of responsibility
for the 101st Airborne
Regiments at Bastogne:

501st Regiment – East
502nd Regiment – West
506th Regiment – North
327th Glider Infantry - South

N

Not to scale

Close calls and near misses accounted for whether some paratroopers came home or not. In Bastogne, narrow escapes were not restricted to the front lines. Tree blasts from artillery strikes took a heavy toll. As artillery rounds hit treetops and exploded, shrapnel wasn't the only killer. Huge limbs and chunks of wood tore off and became deadly projectiles. They tore into foxholes as expertly as a hand grenade tossed by German forces. If a soldier escaped death from the initial blast, he could still bleed to death from the horrific wounds a large chunk of wood could produce. Either way the Germans produced injuries that would keep another American soldier out of the fight even if they were not killed. The concussion of an exploding round added more injuries, though not usually fatal.

Captain Hugo Sims spent December 24th in a small bedroom above the command post. Other officers had quarters upstairs since the second and third floors were vacant. Artillery and aerial bombing had hit several buildings occupied by headquarters personnel. Men climbed the rickety stairs to collapse in makeshift bunks for some sleep as time allowed. Noise from the fighting, especially the artillery rounds arriving all through the nights went unheard as exhausted men dropped into a deep sleep as their heads hit the packs they used as pillows. Sims went to bed that night tired and weary after several trips out in the front lines again that day.

Shaken awake sometime before daylight, Sims remembered, "I slept like a baby. Didn't hear a thing all night. Somebody was shaking me and telling me to get out of the building. By the time I got the cobwebs out, I heard the men talking about a bomb hitting the building. I put on my coat and went to see what they were talking about. I went upstairs with two men and we saw an unexploded bomb lodged in the floor. It was exactly above my bunk. It had come down through the roof and ceiling of the fourth floor and wedged itself in the steel beams of the floor. I looked at it and decided to get out fast. I guess I was really lucky that night, since I hadn't heard anything when it crashed through the roof." The bomb Sims referred to was an unexploded 500 pound bomb dropped from a German fighter-bomber aircraft on the night of December 24, the same bomb referred to in official history records of the 501st PIR. Sims would never have returned home from that Christmas Eve attack if the bomb had exploded on contact as it was designed.

Sims changed jobs at Bastogne. He was given his own company, Company A of the First Battalion. He had proven himself an able leader and was fully ready and qualified when the promotion came down. His days and nights in a covered room near headquarters were at an end. The typical company in the 501st had three platoons, each with approximately 60 men and two officers. Sims thought back over his roster and said, "I had some real good men in my company. Like any paratrooper company, we had our share of real go-getters and a few who needed a little urging to get moving. I don't remember one single problem paratrooper in the company."

With Christmas at hand, Sims took time to write home, even though there was little hope that mail could get out of Bastogne. Still, it was Christmas and he was writing as much for his peace of mind as for his family back home. No holiday atmosphere hung over Bastogne. There were no festive moods, only the feelings of loneliness and homesickness. For the surrounded paratroopers it became a time to wish, to wish they were anywhere but Bastogne. The battle raged on as Christmas neared.

Artillery attacks came at all hours. Not as many frontal assaults by German forces, but many small unit thrusts and harassing artillery fire erupted around the perimeter. Germans did attack in the northern sector near Noville and Foy, pushing the ring around Bastogne tighter. The highway between was vital to German objectives and for the Allies to defend and German forces were determined to possess and control that road. In so doing, they could ill afford to let Allied forces control Foy or Noville.

General Middleton knew the northern sector was vital and under heavy threat of being overrun. He ordered the 101st to control the sector around Noville and Foy. The job was given to the 506th Regiment and began to unravel almost as quickly as it started. German forces had superior armor and motorized artillery coming in from up north. The German tanks were placed in the attack to give German infantry an edge in firepower. Tanks preceded the infantry, much as they had on the eastern side of Bastogne against Ewell's First Battalion when the paratroopers first arrived in Bastogne. As the tanks moved forward, the infantry followed. Troops were fanned out in skirmish lines bringing frontal assaults against American positions.

The paratroopers had no choice but to withdraw and regroup. They were outnumbered and out-gunned. Each small concession in territory gave German forces added confidence. American losses were not high in numbers but each move back towards Bastogne produced a sour taste in the mouths of paratroopers. They didn't want to concede one inch of ground, but the tactics of the commanding officers won out and the withdrawal continued.

As the German ring tightened, the paratroopers formed new defensive perimeter bands around Bastogne. Before new ammo and supplies were dropped on the 23rd, a new firing tactic for the artillery units defending the town was devised. With only 10 rounds a day to fire, it was decided to pull the artillery units into the town, and then deploy them out to a specific location where the Germans attacked. Upon completion of that particular assignment, the artillery unit would hastily retreat back into the town to be ready to move out in another direction when needed. This turned out to be a brilliant maneuver. German units thought there was a much larger artillery force under Allied command than previously expected. Had the Germans attacked from multiple directions at the same time, the battle at Bastogne would most likely have had a much different outcome.

Sims recalled the maneuvering, "I don't know who came up with that plan, but I ran into artillery units coming and going to their locations almost by the hour. It made me believe we had more big guns just by seeing so many moving around. German rounds were coming in all hours of the day and night. The town was torn to pieces by Christmas."

The chapel was being used as a field hospital. Doctors and medics fought a lack of medical supplies. The Division surgeon and most of his staff and supplies had been captured by the Germans. Sims passed in and out of the chapel almost daily. "Some wounded men were laying on makeshift bunks, others on blankets on the concrete floor. Doctors could only do so much with their limited drugs and supplies. Some wounded were going to die because their wounds were too serious to be treated. The doctors had to focus on the ones they could save." Hugo's eyes looked down as he shook his head, "I can still see one wall where six men were laying beside each other, and I knew they wouldn't make it. One of them was crying softly, asking for help. A medic sat beside him, I guess to comfort the soldier, but there was nothing else the medic could do but be there. That's a sad picture I still carry."

Medics scurried around to gather clothing and cover for the wounded. As a man died, his clothing, blankets and boots became part of the supply chain. The dead were taken outside to make room for those wounded coming in. Above everything aside from their wounds was the cold. Everybody was cold in the chapel. Parts of the roof were gone and the cold December wind swirled inside and out. After the resupply drop on December 23, the doctors finally received drugs and supplies they desperately needed. Wounded men could then have more drugs to relieve the pain.

By late December, Patton arrived with his tanks and support elements. German activity was cast into a role of defeat and retreat. With the Allied win at Bastogne, Hitler's plan to regain the upper hand was a complete failure.

OPERATION OSCAR

ALSACE-LORRAINE

OPERATION OSCAR

"If everyone is moving forward together,
then success takes care of itself."
Henry Ford

I n early January of 1945, Hugo's unit was sent to Alsace-Lorraine. German forces had initiated an attack on the Allies at the Saverne Pass. The 442nd Infantry Division had suffered heavy casualties and the 501st was dispatched to help relieve them. Most thought the war was in the final stages, especially since the Allies had the Germans in retreat. German forces were being pushed towards the homeland, but they fought all the way. It looked like only the final thrust into Germany to defeat Hitler remained.

Sims recalled the transport by truck, "We loaded into open top trailers pulled by the cab portion of what today is an eighteen wheeler. That trip was worse than the one we took going into Bastogne. The weather was cold and damp. Wind whistled and swirled in those trailers and the floors were made of metal, and they were cold. The roads were full of potholes and bumps. We were miserable."

Most of the 501st were by now hardened veterans, but a few new paratroopers were shipped in to fill out their ranks. The officer corps led by example, much like they had in Normandy and Holland. Many enlisted men, especially the sergeants, were now fully capable of leading in combat. The entire 101st Division was as experienced as any fighting unit in the Allied Command.

The 501st had a destination on the west bank of the Moder River, north of Strasbourg, Germany. German forces occupied the east bank of the Moder and were firmly entrenched. The river was moderately shallow, but in periods of heavy rains it could become too deep to wade across. The rocky bottom was one with potholes from swirling water. That section of Alsace-Lorraine was in mountainous terrain, with some sectors in undulating hills leading up to higher elevations.

Sims had his entire new Company A in the trek. Not having been the CO very long, he didn't know all the men personally yet. He had fought alongside them in previous battles, but not as their commander. He smiled in recalling, "I had a good Company. I was getting to know them as time went on. Oh, there were a few hard cases, not really serious problems. Just a little matter here and there. A few complained about most anything, but that was about all. When taken as a whole they were as good a unit as we had in the Regiment. They followed orders. They fought well as a unit. They worked well as a team."

By the last of January, Sims was called into Regimental Headquarters. There he received orders that his A Company would be first out in an operation on the 31st of January. "I was told it was Operation Oscar", he said, "and we would be leading a diversionary action. I wasn't told about any other details of the operation, just that I was to move out with my Company, Company B and Company E of the 327th. They showed me on the map where we would be going. We were to proceed towards a large patch of woods across the Moder River. We were to cross the river, cross one small open field, go through the woods, clearing out any Germans, and link up with another unit on the other side and return with prisoners if we could capture some."

Hugo was silent a moment before speaking again, "Speed was going to be necessary. We wanted to have surprise on our side. I gathered the Company and told them that we would move fast and if anyone was wounded or got killed, we would not stop. but leave them and come back for them later. A few men didn't like that. I didn't either, but that's what I was told to do, and under the circumstances it was our best opportunity to succeed. We didn't know the German strength and we didn't have a lot of back-up, so speed was our best selection."

The engineers built a walkway bridge over the shallow Moder and Sims led his Company across the river, then through the open field and started towards the tree line in darkness. Passing into the woods quietly, Sims received the signal to withdraw. He would return in a predestinated route. Sims spoke, "When the signal to withdraw was given, we were ambushed by about a hundred and fifty Germans who had infiltrated into positions between us and the American lines. The only option I had was to rush straight at them."

German machine gun fire erupted from the trees. Instantly Sims led out towards the trees, firing his tommy gun from the hip as he ran. The remainder of his Company immediately joined the frontal attack towards the trees, all firing as they ran. German defenders in the trees found themselves under a savage attack in the night. Sims led Company A into the trees, killing Germans by firing at muzzle flashes from German weapons. His entire Company was cutting down German after German in the dark. Sims recalled, "We killed all of them except for a German officer and about 15 enlisted men that we took back as prisoners."

As General Richard Allen would later recall, "Sims was on a mission. He wiped out a force that outnumbered him two-to-one that night. He executed the plan flawlessly. That was an outstanding job he did that night."

Hugo Sims was awarded the Silver Star for his action in Operation Oscar, and in the same fashion as in patrol, he returned with multiple prisoners. He lost one man who was killed and three were wounded in Operation Oscar. Company B was just as successful as Company A and Operation Oscar was another victory for the Allies.

Operation Oscar was the last significant action for Hugo Sims. World War II would slip into his life in Orangeburg after the war without fanfare. He returned to The United States by transport ship. He returned home a hero for all his deeds in the war. The demure man who left Orangeburg, South Carolina, would once again reflect his unassuming manner, only now he had seen the horror a war has to offer. He would never lose the memories, never forget those who died.

HOME AT LAST

"Do not go where the path may lead,
Instead go where there is no path and leave a trail"
Ralph Waldo Emerson

Sims re-entered civilian life with the same enthusiasm he had displayed in the 101st. He continued his college education and earned his LLB at the University of South Carolina, something he decided to do instead of returning to newspaper work. He practiced law in Orangeburg. He found that he also had a desire to become a real estate broker, investing and developing commercial properties, so he obtained his broker's license. Sims bought an apartment complex in Florida and converted it into condos, allowing tenants to purchase their apartments. He turned a healthy profit in the endeavor and expanded to buying and selling properties in South Carolina, Georgia, and Florida. This was a pattern he followed for 18 years after the war.

Hugo entered politics and was elected to the US House of Representatives. At the age of 28 he was the youngest Representative in history. He also served in the South Carolina Legislature representing Orangeburg County for two years. He went on to found the Orangeburg National

Bank and was selected to be the Chairman of the Board and CEO for many years. In 1991, Hugo received an honorary degree of Doctor of Law from Wofford College, his alma mater, where he later served on the Wofford Board of Trusties for 12 years.

His public and community service did not stop there. Sims was a delegate to two General Conferences of the United Methodist Church, and served as a Trustee of the Orangeburg District, South Carolina Conference, United Methodist Church. He also served on the Board of Trustees Advisory Council of Claflin College in Orangeburg, on the Advisory Committee of Emory University in Atlanta, Georgia, and on the Advisory Committee of Columbia College in Columbia, South Carolina.

In addition, he served as the past president of Orangeburg Rotary Club, was active in the Orangeburg chapter of the American Red Cross, the Orangeburg District of the Boy Scouts of America, and was the campaign chairman of the United Fund. He also received the Kiwanis Club's Outstanding Man of the Year award.

Many people have expressed praise on Hugo following his military service. Newspapers have written of his exploits many times. He led in his community, his town, his state and his nation. Most people never get that chance, and when they do, most fall short when compared to Hugo Sims. As for his military service, none have said it better than General Richard Allen as written in his Forward in this book. Representative Sam Gibbons, D-Fla, who jumped in Normandy with Sims and the paratroopers, said of Hugo, "He was the bravest soldier I ever worked with." Enough said.

Sims comes home

Hugo returned home to Orangeburg after World War
ll as a decorated Captain in the 101st Airborne Division.
During the war, Sims earned the nation's second
highest award for bravery in combat, the Distinguished
Service Cross, as well as the Silver Star and the Bronze
Star. France awarded him medals, as did Holland.

Sims Elected Congressman

Hugo Sims' picture is featured on the cover of the Pictorial Directory of the 81st Congress in 1949 after he was elected to represent the 2nd District of South Carolina in the US House of Representatives. (Photo courtesy the Sims Family)

Marathon run at age 59

Hugo completes the Isle of Palms marathon
in South Carolina on December 6, 1980

The Hugo S. Sims Family

Taken in the late 1940's, the family picture was taken
during Hugo's political days. Pictured left to right
Hugo with son Cal on his lap, Virginia, Ginger
and Hugo lll. (Photo courtesy the Sims family)

Return visit to Holland

Hugo and his wife Virginia make a trip to
Holland in 1998 to retrace his steps during
World War ll. (Photo courtesy Sims Family)

Where the Incredible Patrol began

Hugo revisits the site where the Incredible
Patrol jumped off to cross the river to start
the now famous mission. Note the monument
erected by Holland marking the location for
history. (Photo courtesy Sims family)

EPILOGUE

Hugo Sheridan Sims, Jr., and I met in late 1978. My family and I had just moved to Orangeburg, SC, from Florida. Hugo was a member of the church we visited and one of the first to welcome my family and me.

As time moved forward, I began to discover more information about Hugo and his history. A local newspaper article about Hugo and some of his World War II experiences shed more light on the mild mannered man who sat in the church pew several rows behind us. Having an 8-year background in the US Marine Corps, I had an avid interest in military history. I cornered Hugo many times and asked questions about the events written in that article. Hugo was reluctant to discuss his exploits. I thought perhaps his reluctance was due to the short time we had to speak after church services. I later learned the real reason he appeared reluctant was due to his personality. Hugo always minimized the importance of his involvement; shifting the focus to others. He was a quiet and reserved individual, who preferred not to be in the limelight.

A few years passed and our friendship grew. I suggested that his story should be told and I had an interest in writing it. I had already had one book published and he knew that. Still, he didn't relent. He claimed his daughter had been pushing to write about him, so he wasn't interested at the time. The more my research uncovered about Hugo the more I became convinced that his was a story that should be published. The years passed without his acquiescing.

I kept after Hugo for the next several years. Each time, Hugo would smile and turn down the offer. His family supported the concept but Hugo still resisted. Finally Hugo gave in and we discussed the project in detail. I proposed we would meet on a regular basis, at his office or mine, and I would ask questions. I had a general idea of the question line I would pursue. Hugo didn't like the idea of my recording the sessions. He didn't like the way he sounded on tape, but he finally approved my doing it as a matter of accuracy.

For the following three years Hugo and I sat and talked. I saw him deep in concentration at times, talkative in others. I watched his eyes water a time or two at a specific memory and I saw him smile in telling other stories. He tilted his head down, chin almost touching his chest as he recalled the details of the night parachute jump over Normandy and the horrors he watched. I saw him beam as he recounted his feelings at the completion of his Incredible Patrol and the fact that not one man in his patrol was killed or wounded. We reviewed newspaper articles his family saved, including an original issue of *Life Magazine* in which his Incredible Patrol had been published. We reviewed many other publications pertinent to his experiences in Normandy, Holland and Bastogne.

I came away with a renewed admiration for Hugo Sims, and a closer relationship than I ever realized could exist between men of different generations. He and I developed a deep respect for each other as a result of our conversations during those years. Hugo wore glasses that he often took off before leaning back in his office chair to answer. Other times he let them slide down on his nose and looked over the top of the lenses to answer. Often he hesitated in answering and would question me with, "You really want to know that?" I would smile back and reply, "I wouldn't ask if I didn't". Ours became a special bond, one I will always cherish.

Hugo became ill and died before the book could be published. He had some health issues that eventually took his life on Friday, July 9, 2004. I saw him earlier that week. I'm not sure he knew I was in the room, but I touched his shoulder and told him I missed our talks. His funeral was two days later on Sunday, July 11, 2004 at that same St. Andrews United Methodist Church in Orangeburg. The church had standing room only as friends paid their last respects. The burial was in a cemetery a half-mile away and it was raining. The US Army sent a full Honor Guard for their fallen hero. As we all sat under the funeral tent, the rain escalated into a raging thunderstorm that was so loud it drowned out most of what the minister said. Lightning struck nearby and the thunder was so constant and loud the ground shook. The twenty-one-gun salute sounded like it was a mile away instead of twenty yards. A lone bugler sounded Taps, muffled and faint in the howling wind, thunder and lightning. Through tears, I thought Hugo must have believed he was back in Normandy.

Bibliography/Sources

Interviews with Hugo Sims

Interviews with retired Brigadier General Richard J. Allen

Travel to France to retrace Hugo Sims' WW II Normandy steps

Ambrose, Stephen E., *D-Day, June 6, 1944:the climatic battle of World War II*, (Touchstone, Simon & Shuster)

Bando, Mark, *Vanguard of the Crusade - The 101st Airborne Division in World War II*, (Aberjona Press)

Bando, Mark, *101st Airborne, The Screaming Eagles at Normandy*, (MBI Publishing)

Bastable, Jonathan, *Voices From D-Day*, (David & Charles, Cincinnati, 2004)

Cawthorne, Nigel, *D-Day, Dawn of Heroes*, (Arcturus Publishing Ltd., London England, 2004)

Kagan, Neil and Hyslop, Stephen G., *Eyewitness to World War II*, (National Geographic, Washington, DC 2012)

Legg, Rodney, *D-Day Dorset*, (Dorset Publishing Company, Somerset, England, 1994)

Neillands, Robin and Norman, Roderick, *D-Day 1944, Voices From Normandy*, (Weiden and Nicholson, Berkshire, England, 2001)Battle of the Bulge

Potter, Thomas D., *Brave Men of World War II*, (son of PVT George L. Potter, Jr., E Co, 2nd BN, 506th PIR, Feb 43-Nov 45) Copyright 2003

Pimlott, John, *Battle of the Bulge*, (Gallery Books, New York, 1990)

Public Relations Office, *The Epic of the 101st Airborne*, (Auxerre, France, 1945)

Rapport, Leonard and Northwood, Arthur, *Rendezvous With Destiny, A History of the 101st Airborne Division*, (Infantry Journal Press, Washington, 1948)

Webster, David Kenyon, *Parachute Infantry*, (Dell Publishing, New York, 1994)

Records Division - Offices of the War Cabinet, Washington, DC

Books and periodicals

UNITED STATES ARMY IN WORLD WAR II: The European Theater of Operations, CROSS CHANNEL ATTACK, by Gordon A. Harrison, Office of the Chief of Military History, Department of the Army, Washington, D.C., 1951

Prepared by Monty "Doc" White (The Cleveland Free-Net - aa201) Distributed by the Cybercasting Services Division of the National Public Telecomputing Network (NPTN). Permission is hereby granted to download, reprint, and/or otherwise redistribute this file, provided appropriate point of origin credit is given to the preparer(s) and the National Public Telecomputing Network.

Slayden, Col. William M., *A World War II Expeience, The Battle of the Bulge*, (US Army Center, Washington, DC)

From the US Army Center for Military History, Washington, DC

- CROSS-CHANNEL ATTACK, by Gordon A. Harrison. (1951, 1989, 2002; 519 pp., charts, maps, illustrations, appendixes, bibliographical note, glossaries, index). CMH Pub 74; CMH Pub 7-4-1. This first European Theater of Operations tactical volume covers the prelude to the 6 June 1944 assault and combat operations of the First U.S. Army in Normandy to 1 July 1944.

- UTAH BEACH TO CHERBOURG, 6—27 JUNE 1944 (1947, facsimile reprint 1984, 1990, 1994; 213 pp., illustrations, maps, appendixes). CMH Pub 100-12. A companion volume to *Omaha Beachhead*, this narrative rounds out the account of the landings at corps level and below and relates the course of VII Corps combat operations which resulted in the capture of Cherbourg on 27 June 1944.

- BASTOGNE: THE FIRST EIGHT DAYS, by S.L.A. Marshall. (1946, facsimile reprint 1988, 1996; 261 pp., maps, illustrations, appendix, key to notes). CMH Pub 22-2. An account of the defense of Bastogne during the Battle of the Bulge based primarily on interviews with the participants.

- OMAHA BEACHHEAD (1945, facsimile reprint 1984, 1989, 1994, 2001; 167 pp., illustrations, maps, annexes). CMH Pub 100-11-1. An operational account of a major phase of the campaign in Normandy between 6 and 13 June 1944

- COMMAND DECISIONS, ed. Kent Roberts Greenfield. (1960, 1987, 1990, 2002; 565 pp., maps, chronology, glossaries, index). CMH Pub 70-7; CMH Pub 70-7-1. An analysis of 23 decisions reached by chiefs of state and their military subordinates during World War II. Concerned with important political, strategic, tactical, and logistical questions, they include the invasions of North Africa and Normandy, the use of the atomic bomb, the capture of Rome, the campaigns in the western Pacific, and the internment of Japanese-Americans.

- NORMANDY, by William M. Hammond. CMH Pub 72-18, GPO S/N 008-029-00274-4.

- ARDENNES-ALSACE, by Roger Cirillo. CMH Pub 72-26, GPO S/N 008-029-00299-0.

- THE ARDENNES: BATTLE OF THE BULGE, by Hugh M. Cole. (1965, 1983, 1988, 1994; 720 pp., maps, illustrations, appendixes, bibliographical note, glossary, index). CMH Pub 7-8, CMH Pub 7-8. The German winter counteroffensive of December 1944-January 1945 with a detailed description of German plans and Allied efforts to eliminate the bulge in their lines.

- THE SIEGFRIED LINE CAMPAIGN, by Charles B. MacDonald. (1963, 1984, 1990, 2001; 670 pp., maps, illustrations, appendixes, bibliographical note, glossaries, index). CMH Pub 7-7; CMH Pub 7-7-1. The story of the First and Ninth U.S. Armies from the first crossings of the German border in September 1944 to the enemy's counteroffensive in the Ardennes in December, including the reduction of Aachen, Huertgen Forest, and Operation MARKET-GARDEN in Holland.

- *CMH Pub 7-8-1 (Maps) A Portfolio of Maps Extracted from *The Ardennes: Battle of the Bulge*

- *CMH Pub 7-4-1 (Maps) A Portfolio of Maps Extracted from *Cross–Channel Attack*

- *CMH Pub 7-5-1 (Maps) A Portfolio of Maps Extracted from *Breakout and Pursuit*

- *CMH Pub 7-9-1 (Maps) A Portfolio of Maps Extracted from *The Last Offensive*

About the Author

Herb Moore resides near Orangeburg, 25 miles outside the South Carolina capital city of Columbia. Raised in Charleston, SC, Moore moved to his present home in 1978. His interest in writing came early but was not put to practice until he wrote his first book.

Moore served in the US Marine Corps from 1961 to 1968. His military service provided a background for him to write his first book, Rows of Corn, a nonfiction account of Marine Corps basic training Moore endured during the hot summer of 1963.

It was while promoting his first book that Moore appeared on numerous television talk shows throughout the country, as well as on South Carolina ETV programs for writer forums. Moore states his feelings as, "I really don't care to talk about me. I'm not too interesting but I am thrilled to talk about the people I write about. History is full of exciting people with really amazing pasts."

Moore went on to author nonfiction magazine feature articles about interesting people he has met, such as the well-known artist Jim Harrison and internationally famous knife designer Blackie Collins. Moore also wrote feature articles about places, such as the world's longest black water river, the Edisto River.

Moore attended college at the University of South Carolina and Charleston Southern University. He and his wife, Kathy, were high school sweethearts and have two sons, Jeffrey (wife Inna with 2 children, Silas and Addie), and Greg (wife Molly and 2 children, Isaac and Elijah). Herb states, "Kathy and I live in the country on 30 acres with horses, dogs and cats roaming about freely. There is always a fence to mend and never time to do it all, but its home and we love it in the country."

Printed in the United States
By Bookmasters